Praise for *Who Killed Jesus?*

"A book sure to generate both conversation and controversy . . . Well argued and highly readable."

—*Publishers Weekly*

"[An] extraordinary book . . . [Crossan] pleads for a reevaluation of the passion stories, which have caused such animus toward Jews for the past 2000 years. An excellent study."

—*Library Journal*

"Anyone concerned with the rising tide of anti-Semitism in our world, anyone fascinated by the origins of Christianity, and anyone who likes a good mystery will love this book."

—Susannah Heschel,
Case Western Reserve University,
Author of *On Being a Jewish Feminist*

"John Dominic Crossan's account of the story of Jesus is intellectually convincing and brilliantly written. . . . This book deals with large issues. It is essential reading."

—Arthur Hertzberg,
Professor Emeritus of Religion, Dartmouth College

Praise for *Jesus: A Revolutionary Biography*

"Crossan paints his Jesus with great warmth and power. He achieves a portrait that both takes in the contemporary background yet accounts for Jesus' distinctiveness."

—*The New York Times Book Review*

"This is an extremely interesting, erudite, informative, must-read for anyone interested in the New Testament. . . . Read it."

—*National Catholic Reporter*

"This is an outstanding book—both popular and intelligent. . . . Crossan emphasizes that a Christian's current relationship to Christ is enhanced through reconstruction of Jesus' past. We are fortunate to have a writer and a scholar of Crossan's abilities to lead us in that reconstruction."

—*Publishers Weekly*

"Crossan has accomplished something I hardly believed possible. . . . His vivid account, based on state-of-the-art historical and textural analysis, brings Jesus alive in a vibrant and plausible way for the non-specialist."

—Harvey Cox,
Harvard University Divinity School

"The book is marvelous. Crossan's respect for both memory and imagination lets him paint a portrait of Jesus even while dismantling the mythic materials of the gospels. The style is dazzling; the portrait haunting."

—Burton Mack,
Author of *The Lost Gospel*

Praise for *The Historical Jesus*

"Crossan's book is the one I've been looking for for ten years and have never found. It is elegant, even masterful. There is just nothing like it for thoroughness, readability, balance, fairness, and clarity. . . . He delivers the goods."

—Harvey Cox,
Harvard University Divinity School

"Brilliant, the most important book about Jesus in decades."

—Marcus Borg,
Author of *Jesus: A New Vision*

"Adds color to the interpretation of faith."

—Mary Martin,
Author of *Cry of Absence*

"Lively and idiosyncratic in the great tradition of the historical Jesus genre begun by Schweitzer."

—*Christian Science Monitor*

WHO IS JESUS?

Answers to Your Questions about the Historical Jesus

John Dominic Crossan
with Richard G. Watts

HarperPaperbacks
A Division of HarperCollinsPublishers

HarperPaperbacks

A Division of HarperCollins*Publishers*
10 East 53rd Street, New York, N.Y. 10022-5299

Cover illustration: Giraudon/Art Resource, N.Y.
Courtesy of Musee des Beaux-Arts, France.

First printing: December 1996

Printed in the United States of America

Visit HarperPaperbacks on the World Wide Web at
http://www.harpercollins.com/paperbacks

❖ 10 9 8 7 6 5 4 3 2

Dedicated
to the
New Covenant Community
Normal, Illinois

Acknowledgments

We are grateful to Sarah Crossan who organized hundreds of letters to select and edit those used in this book.

We are grateful to members of the New Covenant Community Church of Normal, Illinois, and others organized by Dick Watts to discuss this book in the various stages of its formation: Pat Abell, Jean Bates, Jim Bortell, Jim Boswell, Julia Cisco, Raydean Davis, Joel Erickson, Willemina Esenwein, Colleen Farlee, Lloyd Farlee, Ann Farnsworth, Randy Gibson, Anita Gilmore, Hal Gilmore, Cheri Grizzard, Julie Jarvis, Mike Kelleher, Otta Key, Dorothy Lee, Caryl Lemke, Skip Lemke, Pam Lewis, Dick LeMoine, Merrilee LeMoine, Cynthia Ashbrook Maurer, Elleke Mesdag, Bill Moonan, Ed Nestingen, Laura Pedrick, Gwen Pruyne, Jim Pruyne, Betty Rademacher, David Rademacher, Jim Roderick, Vera Roderick, Jean Rogers, Margaret Rutter, Russ Rutter, Katie Sawyer, Garrett Scott, Sandy Scott, Jody Stewart, Jerry Stone, Judy Stone, Bill Tolone, Kathy Vitek, Lloyd Watkins, Mary Watkins, Charline Watts, Art White, and Mark Wyman.

We are grateful to Kathy Vitek, not only for her participation in that discussion group, but also for her word processing skills used in the development of this book.

CONTENTS

Why This Book?

"**S**cholar Refutes Jesus Stories." That was the headline to a front-page newspaper story about a speech I recently gave in a Midwestern university town. That headline, and the story that followed, ignited a firestorm of controversy that raged in the Letters to the Editor pages for the next six weeks. Opinions ranged from "His views are so far out that I can't believe he says he's a Christian" to calling my approach "a way of fully appreciating the richness and beauty of the Gospels, in our 20th century context." So which is it? Is my search for the historical Jesus a threat to faith? Or does it help make faith a possibility for modern men and women?

Actually, that headline writer got it wrong. My purpose was to try to *understand* the stories of Jesus, not *refute* them. The title of my speech that evening was simply "What I've Learned from Thirty-Five Years of Searching for the Historical Jesus." And that is also what this book is about. It is an invitation to journey back in time with me to see Jesus in his own setting in the first-century Jewish homeland. But before we begin, let me tell you a bit about myself and how I got involved in this search.

I grew up in small towns in Ireland. In 1950, at the age of sixteen, I entered the Servites, a Roman Catholic monastic order founded in the thirteenth century. That was the century when Saint Thomas Aquinas combined Aristotle's philosophy with Catholic theology, and never worried that one might contradict the other. Reason and revelation, he insisted, were twin gifts from the same God, and could not be in conflict—unless we misunderstood one or both of them.

That same conviction was deeply embedded in my own heart when, after six years of studying philosophy and theology, I was ordained a priest in 1957. My priestly life was spent more in the library than the parish, and included years of advanced study at the Pontifical Biblical Institute in Rome and the French School of Archaeology in Jerusalem. As a priest, I taught in a number of colleges, universities, and seminaries in the Chicago area.

In 1969 I asked for and received permission to leave the priesthood and the Servite Order. I left primarily in order to marry, but also to avoid a conflict of interest between priestly loyalty and scholarly honesty. The official letter of permission from the Vatican was dated July Fourth—which I considered rather appropriate. Did I leave with feelings of resentment and anger toward the Church? No. While I was a monk and a priest, I was quite happy. When I was no longer happy, I left. It was that simple. Some others have been badly hurt in such transitions; I was not.

From those years in that medieval order I have retained three rather medieval gifts. The first is my name: John is my civil name, and Dominic the new name given me when I entered the Servites. The second is a profound conviction that faith and fact, revelation and reason cannot contradict one another, unless the human mind has misunderstood either or both. The third gift is a very great love for Gregorian Chant, which I sang badly enough to ruin whole choirs and for whose survival my departure was probably a public service.

After leaving the priesthood in 1969, I joined the faculty of DePaul University in Chicago, remaining there until my retirement as Professor Emeritus in 1995. Since I have been a religiously controversial figure, that long tenure is a tribute to the courage and integrity for which DePaul has long stood.

When I joined DePaul, I needed to choose a research focus. At the seminary I had been teaching courses on the parables of Jesus and on the resurrection stories, so I decided to concentrate on the historical Jesus. Year after year I researched and published on particular aspects of Jesus as seen in his own historical context. Indeed, I am probably the only scholar in the world who has spent an entire lifetime on the search for the historical Jesus. That, of course, does not necessarily make me right—but it does makes my opinions worth considering.

In 1985 I joined with Robert Funk, newly retired from the University of Montana, in founding the Jesus Seminar, a group of scholars interested in questions of historical Jesus research and Christian origins. The Jesus Seminar usually involves some forty or fifty scholars at four-day sessions held twice a year. What has brought us a lot of public attention is that we not only discuss, we *decide*. Suppose, for example, that we are working together on a subject like the "Kingdom of God" sayings attributed to Jesus in the Gospels. After extensive debate, we vote in secret, using colored beads to indicate our views about how likely it is that the particular words actually came from the historical Jesus. A red bead means that the saying "most likely" came from Jesus, a pink bead means "likely," a gray bead means "not likely," and a black bead means "very unlikely." Although such voting has attracted a lot of media attention, there is really nothing unusual about it. For example, you may have in your home a version of the New Testament which often has footnotes to a particular verse, saying something like, "Other ancient authorities read . . ." That means that a committee of scholars, looking at ancient manuscripts that are different from each other, have voted on which is most authentic—a process much like ours in the Jesus Seminar.

What has made the Jesus Seminar notorious is that *we do our work out in the open, inviting media attention, letting anyone who is interested in on our processes as well as our conclusions.* We do not want to hide our work in scholarly journals, writing only for one another. We want to let the general public know what we are doing, and to invite them to join the dialogue on major issues of Jesus research.

Besides my work with the Jesus Seminar, during the 1980s I continued to publish the results of my own research, basically for other scholars. But then an amazing thing happened. In 1991 I published *The Historical Jesus: The Life of a Mediterranean Jewish Peasant*, a major summary of my research into Jesus' life and work. I assumed that other scholars would read it, and that the general public would never even hear of it. But Peter Steinfels of *The New York Times* mentioned it in a front-page article around Christmastime, and his story was picked up by many other newspapers. By June, to my great surprise, the book was at the top of *Publishers Weekly* religious bestseller list. A briefer version, *Jesus: A Revolutionary Biography*, was on the same top-ten list for eight months in 1994. (It was pushed downwards by the new *Catechism of the Catholic Church*, which proves that God has a sense of humor.) The unexpected popularity of these books shows a deep and widespread public interest in the figure of Jesus.

Which brings us to the question: Why *this* book?

The answer has three parts. First, there is a need for a brief, easily read introduction to basic questions and conclusions of Jesus research for general readers. Not everyone has the background to plow through dense thickets of scholarly argument. This book is meant to make sense to you, even if you have never studied the Bible or had a course on Christian origins. Second, in recent years I have done nearly a hundred radio talk shows and probably as many newspaper interviews, and from those have learned a lot about the questions that are on people's minds. This book is written in a question-and-answer style, not only to break up the text into bite-sized chunks, but to give me a chance to answer typical questions. Third, I have received hundreds of letters—from thirty-eight states and twenty foreign countries—from people who have read my books, heard me speak, or read media reviews of my work. This book not only lets me answer them, but also gives you a chance to see what others are thinking and saying. Each chapter begins with selections from typical letters, edited down for reasons of space. By the way, I expected negative letters; it is the positive ones that surprised me. For each letter that accuses me of betraying the faith, I get four to five others that thank me for helping the writers reconnect with the historical Jesus and their Christian faith. I am very grateful to these letter writers for their questions and concerns, whether in agreement or disagreement with my own positions. Although I could not reply adequately to each one, this book includes a large sampling of letters in an effort to respond finally to them all. In short then, this book is intended to make the results of a lifetime of scholarship about the historical Jesus readily available to a wide audience of nonspecialists.

I send this book out with confidence that it will be useful, because many people have been discussing draft versions and helping to shape its final form. I am grateful to Dick Watts, who suggested this book, "translated" my scholarly work into everyday language, and gathered groups of interested people to wrestle with my conclusions. Most of them are participants in a parish church, the New Covenant Community of Normal, Illinois, to whom the book is dedicated.

WHO IS JESUS?

1

Why Not Just Read the Gospels?

For many years I have been looking for such a book [as Jesus: A Revolutionary Biography], so much of what I knew about Jesus just didn't "ring true" and yet there was always a slight fear that I might be in some way denying a faith instilled as a child and certainly entrenched in the early years of religious life. Your book . . . has reinforced my own belief that growing involves "unlearning" as well as learning and that this can be very positive and even exciting. . . . Rather than diminish my faith and love for Jesus your book has surely strengthened it and opened up a whole new appreciation of what it means to be a follower of his.

A woman from Massachusetts

You must be a lucky person to get paid to SEARCH, and to be able to SEARCH as part of your everyday life. . . . I'm going on age fifty-two having done little SEARCH . . . maybe I should begin a SEARCH that might make my religion somewhat meaningful. I was forced into baptism, forced through a program of much religious indoctrination and sacraments in

Catholic schools. . . . I must take some initiative, away from force, and away from the expectations of others, in pursuit of a God other than this GOD *of force. . . . What is more important . . . that we search or that we are satisfied with our answers?*

A man from Wisconsin

Your book, The Historical Jesus: The Life of a Mediterranean Jewish Peasant, *has been "our" quest this fall ("our" meaning a bunch of pew-piles looking through glasses darkly for any Jesus at all). We feel bonded to you as our guru in absentia.*

A group from North Carolina

Many people believe that religious faith and science are incompatible—the more you know, the less faith you will have. . . . I assume that you are a man of faith. And as someone who was once an orthodox Catholic who would like to have more faith . . . I have read just enough of the Bible to confuse me. . . . [I write to you] as someone who seeks plausible explanations for what seem to me confusing and conflicting passages. . . .There are many passages that are troubling to those of us who are inquisitive enough to ask questions, but perhaps not smart enough to figure out how to reconcile these passages. But, you must have reconciled these passages with your Catholic faith. But, how?

A man from California

There is definitely a need for a religion that is believable by an intelligent contemporary person with a general background in the sciences. There isn't anything out there that is trying to answer that need.

A man from Massachusetts

I thank Crossan and theologians like him for assuming that I have brains and heart enough to mature with my faith, putting away the storybook and childish interpretations that any close, clearheaded reading of the gospels simply cannot, nor, as I believe, intend to sustain. . . . The bottom line is, if my faith cannot withstand intellectual waves and winds, then, as a Christian, what am I doing in the boat anyway?

A woman from Illinois

One thing I do not understand is how can you and other members of the Jesus Seminar vote on what words Jesus actually said. Is this something you should be voting about? How can you say that some of what the Bible says is true and other things are not?

A woman from Illinois

Why is research on the historical Jesus necessary at all? Don't we already have four biographies of Jesus—by Matthew, Mark, Luke, and John? With four separate biographies in front of us, what's the problem?

Actually, the fact that we have four gospels lies at the very heart of our problem. Because as we read particular parables or sayings or stories in several different versions, we can't miss the *disagreements* between them. At first we are tempted to say, "Well, witnesses simply remember the same things differently." But it is clear that, when Matthew and Luke wrote their gospels, they had copies of Mark (the earliest of the New Testament gospels) in front of them. That means that for much of their story of Jesus, Matthew and Luke are not *independent* sources, but *variations* of Mark. It also means that the variations reflect the theologies of the individual gospel writers. In other words, each gospel is a deliberate *interpretation* of Jesus—rather than a biography.

There is a second problem. Those four gospels are not the only ones written about Jesus. Other gospels are found, either hidden within the four we have in the New Testament or discovered outside them. An example of the first sort is the reconstructed document known as Q. That designation comes from the German word "*Quelle*," which means "source." That text is embedded within both Luke and Matthew, in material common to both of them but not present in Mark. Because I think of that source not just as filler, but as a gospel with its own distinctive theology, I will refer to it throughout this book as the Q *Gospel*.

An example of a document found *outside* Matthew, Mark, Luke, and John is the *Gospel of Thomas*, which was found in Egypt in 1945. It is, in my view, completely independent of the four New Testament gospels. It is also very different from them in its format—in fact, it is much more like the Q *Gospel*. It is basically a collection of the *sayings* of

Jesus without any stories of deeds or miracles, or crucifixion or resurrection.

With all of the differences between Matthew, Mark, Luke, and John and with numerous other gospels existing, we have an obvious problem. Each gospel has a particular way of seeing Jesus. How close to the historical facts are they?

Is there any way to get behind the interpretations to see the Jesus who actually lived?

Many scholarly tools are available to help in that task, and many attempts have been made to paint a picture of the historical Jesus. Some of those pictures are persuasive; some are highly imaginative. Clearly, everything depends upon the methods used to uncover the facts about Jesus. Therefore, I want to clarify at the outset my method for reconstructing the historical Jesus.

I liken my method to three giant searchlights coming together on a single object in the night sky. Each one of the searchlights must strike the object at the same place. Since all three of my "searchlights" must intersect at the same point for any of them to be correct, each serves to correct the other two. Where all three intersect I have a high degree of confidence that they are focused on the historical Jesus.

My first searchlight is *cross-cultural study*. This discipline helps me learn as much as I possibly can about the social setting in which Jesus lived. What I do is look at all of the societies across history that are similar to his. I ask, for example, what I can learn about

ancient Mediterranean cultures—as distinct, say, from
contemporary American culture. How does an agrarian
society differ from an industrial society? What can I
learn about phenomena we find in the gospel stories—
evil spirits, healing, exorcism? What can scholars tell
me about societies that, like the one in which Jesus
lived, have elites and peasants, colonial subjects and
imperial rulers? What in such a society are politics and
family, tax and debt, class and gender relations like?
The value of this sort of study is that it has no direct
connection with the gospel pictures of Jesus and is,
therefore, not likely to be skewed for or against him.
To take an example: If I am tempted to picture Jesus as
a literate, middle class carpenter, cross-cultural study
reminds me that no middle class existed in ancient
societies and that the peasant class from which he
came is largely illiterate. So I am kept from imagining a
Jesus who could not possibly have existed at his time
and in his situation.

My second searchlight is *historical study* about
Greco-Roman and Jewish affairs in Jesus' time. We
know a great deal about the situation of the Jewish
homeland as a colony of the Roman Empire, ruled
either directly by Roman governors or indirectly by the
House of Herod. I give special attention to a first-century
Jewish historian named Josephus, who wrote two separate but overlapping accounts of that period. Jesus
lived amid an undercurrent of peasant unrest and agi-
tation in a land where revolution was just waiting for a
chance to happen. And so I listen very carefully to
what Josephus tells me about protesters and prophets,
bandits and messiahs. If I am to get a true picture of

Jesus, I must try to imagine the story of peasant unrest that smolders beneath the surface and never gets recorded until it bursts forth openly into rebellion.

The third searchlight is *textual study*. This is the most difficult part of the quest for the historical Jesus. I have already mentioned that textual study involves sifting through gospels not only within, but also outside of the New Testament. But it also means that I have to try to distinguish between *three levels* of the literary tradition. At the first level the tradition retains sayings and happenings that go back to the historical Jesus. At the second level those retained materials are developed—for example, by weaving stories around originally isolated sayings. The third level involves creating totally new stories and sayings which are then put in the mouth of Jesus.

If you have ever read a newspaper story about a priceless old master painting found in somebody's attic, which had been covered over by later paintings, you have some idea of what textual study is like. Just as the art museum curator goes to work with delicate tools and chemicals to try to remove the overlay and uncover the original masterpiece, so scholars use a variety of sophisticated methods to get down through the layers of interpretation to the original picture of Jesus.

Are you saying that the gospel writers didn't tell the truth?

Sometimes people are shocked at the notion that Matthew, Mark, Luke, and John might have elaborated upon actual events or even created stories and sayings about Jesus from scratch. We need to understand that the first Christians experienced Jesus as continuing to be present with them after he died. That sense of continued presence gave the transmitters of the Jesus tradition a creative freedom. They did not write so much about the Jesus who *was*, but the Jesus who *is*; not the Jesus who *said*, but the Jesus who *says*; not the Jesus who *did*, but the Jesus who *does*. So they were unembarrassed to restate the words and deeds of Jesus in ways that met the particular needs of their own times and communities. When, therefore, I talk about getting behind the gospels to the historical Jesus, I am not denying the value of the gospels as they stand. What I am saying is simply that they are neither histories nor biographies, but interpretations for particular times, places, and communities. In order to see the historical Jesus, we need to get behind those interpretations.

One final point about my method. In an effort to paint a picture of the real Jesus, I pay most attention to the earliest layer of the tradition—materials dating between the years 30 and 60 of the first century—and to sayings and stories that are found independently in more than one source from those materials. Stories found in only one source of the tradition may, of course, be accurate, but I try to build my picture of Jesus upward from accounts with multiple independent attestations rather than from accounts with only a single independent attestation. That discipline may not guarantee truth but at least makes it more difficult to be innaccurate.

It is very important for me—*to be honest in my search for the historical Jesus.* I have tried to reconstruct the historical Jesus as accurately as possible. It was never my purpose to try to find a Jesus whom I liked or disliked, a Jesus with whom I agreed or disagreed. I do not pretend that I have the final picture of Jesus, but I do offer my reconstruction as an honest one.

I refer those who wish to explore this subject in more detail and would like to know the scholarly evidence upon which my conclusions are based to my earlier books. *The Historical Jesus: The Life of a Mediterranean Jewish Peasant* is the fullest presentation of my argument. *Jesus: A Revolutionary Biography* is a briefer version of that larger volume. My presentation of the original recorded sayings and earliest pictorial images of Jesus is called *The Essential Jesus.* Finally, the roots of anti-Semitism in the gospel story of the death of Jesus are explored in *Who Killed Jesus?*

2

Son of God,
Son of the Virgin Mary?

I was recently released as a bishop in the Church of Jesus Christ of Latter Day Saints. Shortly afterwards I read your book, The Historical Jesus: The Life of a Mediterranean Jewish Peasant. *Thanks for giving me a new insight to the Jesus Christ I love and worship.*

A man from Illinois

[You write] probably for your own glory and monetary gain—certainly not to increase anyone's faith and probably many people who read stuff like that would lose faith and even leave the church. . . . It would seem that anyone with any energy at all would try to do good by working with people when there is so much to be done to bring souls closer to God.

A woman from Florida

I read an article entitled "Scholar Sees Jesus as Revolutionary" in our local newspaper. I was out-

raged at the statements you made. . . . MANY,
MANY born again Christians, along with those Bible
scholars who have made intensive studies of the
Bible, have a much different picture of our Lord than
you have. . . . You state that Christ was an illiterate
peasant, for example. Don't you realize that Christ
was God in human form . . . the one who created
ALL things and that His knowledge did not have to
come from university/theological training! He knew,
and knows ALL things and such knowledge is far
above what you or I or any human could EVER possibly know!

A woman from Indiana

It is the theologians and researchers like yourself
who make my Sunday mornings meaningful. After
our Sunday sessions, the whole class feels more comfortable about facing the polarized world of fundamentalism. Thank you for your work and the work
of the Jesus Seminar. Your research, your interpretations, and your honesty are appreciated.

A woman from Texas

I like your ideas of a wisdom teacher, using
Zenlike aphorisms and puzzling parables to challenge
social conventions. But there is something exceedingly wise and metaphysically true in his teachings,
if the Scriptures have them correct, that makes me
wonder where he got these truths. Could he have
been to India as a youth, or under the tutelage of a
teacher from India?

A man from Missouri

Do you dispute the writings and prophecies of the old prophets that the Virgin would be with child and that Bethlehem, the least of the towns of Judah, would bring forth a leader for all the Israelites (my words)? I don't see anyone trying to change the Old Testament or the prophets' writings! I guess this will be called the "Jesus-Bashing" century.

A man from Florida

I understand you recently participated in the Jesus Seminar and it is alleged in a Toronto Star report that you do not believe in some of the essentials of the Christian faith. . . . I'm afraid we are all a bit late to prove or disprove the authenticity of the Bible—we might just have to accept it by faith, Mr. Crossan! Besides, don't we need Jesus to pay for the wages of our sins? WHY do you disbelieve? What possibly could you gain by denying the essentials of the faith?

A man from Canada

After hearing your interview with Terri Gross on "Fresh Air," I read your book, Jesus: A Revolutionary Biography and enjoyed it very much. Being raised a Catholic in the Boston area, attending Catholic schools, and being an altar boy, I learned a lot about ordinary venial and mortal sin, the stations of the cross, the crown of thorns, purgatory and hell, but nothing about the life of Jesus and his message of absolute equality. In rejecting all I was taught about virgin births, miracles and the resurrection, I never studied further who and what Jesus was.

A man from New Hampshire

What do the birth stories in the gospels tell us about the historical Jesus?

By the "historical Jesus," I mean the real person who walked the dusty roads of Galilee, ate and drank, taught about God's Kingdom, was arrested and executed—so far as historical research can uncover him.

But some of the best-known stories about Jesus do not shed any light on him as a historical figure. I refer to the very familiar nativity stories that we read each Christmas—with Mary and Joseph and the infant Jesus at the manger, surrounded by shepherds, wise men, and angels. The stories of Jesus' birth are religious fiction, or parable, if you prefer. As I will try to show, this does not mean that they have no value, but it does mean that they are not to be read as literal historical fact. Rather, they are like overtures introducing a Broadway musical. An overture catches up the various themes that will be heard throughout the musical. Since Matthew and Luke have produced different versions of the Jesus story, their overtures are different, too.

You said that the story of Jesus' birth is "religious fiction." That must come as quite a shock to most Christian believers. How do you find people reacting to that claim?

Well, the responses are really mixed. Sometimes, of course, I get critical and angry letters either to myself or to newspapers and periodicals that publish my views. On the other hand, I often receive comments from people who express gratitude that they don't need to leave their minds outside the church door when they go to worship. They're grateful to know that it's possible to take the Christian message *seriously* without taking it at all points *literally*.

I assure you that I have no interest in being the Grinch who stole Christmas. I have to be honest as a historian in dealing with the facts as I discover them. But my purpose is a positive one: to present the Jesus who appears to us through the disciplines of historical, literary, and cross-cultural studies. My purpose is not to shock or debunk, but to let the Jesus of history be seen as clearly as possible, apart from theologies about him.

You mentioned that Matthew and Luke tell different birth stories. What are the differences?

If you have a nativity set at home that you put out on the table each Christmastime, it probably centers in a manger—a cattle trough filled with straw in which the infant Jesus rests. Perhaps Mary kneels, while Joseph stands nearby. No doubt there are camels in your nativity set belonging to Wise Men who are offering gifts to the infant. There probably also are cows and donkeys and sheep and shepherds. Perhaps above the rude barn in which the manger is placed, a star is set, an angel figure or two in the background.

In our imaginations we have put the features of two gospels together in one scene. Actually, the two birth stories are very, very different. In Luke's story we have the manger, the shepherds, and the angels. In Matthew's story we have the Wise Men, and they come not to a manger, but to a house. Matthew's story goes on to tell about the Wise Men going to King Herod, who seeks to find out where they can find the child born to be a king. Mary, Joseph, and Jesus flee to Egypt to escape the wrath of Herod, who murders the male children two years old and younger around Bethlehem in an effort to destroy the infant savior. These stories in Matthew have no parallel in Luke.

This chart shows some of the major differences between the two stories, where Matthew and Luke have episodes or settings not found in the other:

MATTHEW	LUKE
Angel appears to Joseph	John's conception and birth
Wise Men from the East	Angel appears to Mary
Infant Jesus in the house	Worldwide census
Herod massacres infants	Angel choir
Jesus is taken to Egypt	Jesus' circumcision
	Prophecies of Anna and Simeon

But we can say even more. The first of the gospels to be written, Mark, upon which both Matthew and Luke depend, has no birth story at all. That gospel begins with Jesus as a grown man going to the River Jordan to be baptized by John. The earliest writings in the New Testament, the letters of Paul, contain no reference to birth stories. And the Gospel of John, rather than telling such stories, begins with a meditation on Jesus as the Word of God. So birth stories are found only in Matthew and Luke, and they are radically different one from another.

What this means is that we do not have a straightforward history. What we have, rather, is what I have likened to musical overtures; that is, prefaces to separate gospels that catch up some of the major themes of those gospels. They tell us very little about the historical circumstances of Jesus' birth. But they tell us a great deal about Luke's and Matthew's views of Jesus' place in the story of his people.

If these stories are not historical, then what is their point anyway?

I begin with the birth story in Luke's gospel. What you notice right away is that it is really a story of *two* births, that of Jesus but also of John the Baptist.

John, we're told, is born of aged parents who have long given up any hope of having children. This story looks back to great heroes of Israel's past—to Isaac, who was born of Abraham and Sarah when they were long past the years of childbearing, and to Samuel, who was born to Hannah as a direct result of God's intervention in answer to this infertile woman's prayer. So what we have is the miracle of birth despite infertility and/or old age. We're being told that John is in the tradition of the great heroes of Israel's faith. The story is a common one: persons recognized as great are given special birth stories. A marvelous life and death gets, in retrospect, a marvelous conception and birth.

The story of Jesus' conception and birth parallels that of John—but with the purpose of showing that Jesus is greater than John. John may be born of infertile and aged parents, but Jesus is born of a virgin mother. John's birth is publicized among his neighbors, but Jesus' birth is publicized by a multitude of angels. John's name is specially given to his mother and father after his birth, but Jesus' name is given by an angel before his conception. John is presented publicly and announced as a prophet of the Most High; Jesus is presented in the Temple (rather than just in a home), and the aged Simeon and Anna prophesy of his coming greatness. John is described as growing and becoming strong in spirit; Jesus is said to become strong, filled with wisdom and the favor of God—and at age twelve he is found in the Temple astonishing teachers with his insight.

So in the story we see Luke's clear purpose: to link John the Baptist to the great heroes of Israel's faith, but also to show that Jesus is far greater than John. Luke's message to his readers is: John is the fulfillment of Israel's past, but the future belongs to Jesus. Matthew has a similar point, but he expresses it in a quite different story.

How exactly is Matthew's story different?

Take a look at the story as Matthew tells it. He also links the birth of Jesus to ancient Jewish traditions—but goes about it in a different way. Whereas Luke linked the birth of John and Jesus to Isaac and

Samuel, Matthew draws parallels between Jesus and
Moses.

You remember that in the Exodus story, Pharaoh,
the ruler of Egypt, tried to exterminate the people of
Israel by commanding that sons born to the Hebrews
be thrown into the Nile River to drown. Moses was
born at that time and was saved when his mother hid
him in a basket near the riverbank, where he was
found and then raised by Pharaoh's own daughter. In
popular versions of the story that were told in Jesus'
time, additional details were added. For example,
Moses did not just happen to be born after the massacre was ordered; rather, the massacre was ordered
specifically to kill Moses. Pharaoh had been warned
that a great leader was about to be born to the
Israelites, and so deliberately set out to destroy him.
Furthermore, while many of the people of Israel
divorced their wives in order to avoid having children
that would be massacred, the father of Moses deliberately chose to conceive a child with his wife because
of a prophecy about the child's future greatness.

As Matthew begins his gospel, he models the Jesus
story on the Moses story. The ruler Herod (like
Pharaoh) is warned that a savior is to be born and,
therefore, sets out to massacre all the children two
years old and younger in the region of Bethlehem to
get at the promised deliverer. Joseph (like Moses'
father) is tempted to divorce his wife, but is told in a
dream about the future greatness of the child, and
instead stays with Mary. Moses eventually leads his
people out of Egypt, but Jesus is rescued from the mur-
derous tyrant, not by fleeing *from* Egypt, but by fleeing

to Egypt with his mother and father. By so closely paralleling the stories of Moses and Jesus, Matthew sends a powerful message: *Jesus is the new and greater Moses*.

Now we can see what is happening in these birth stories. Though Luke and Matthew created completely different infancy stories, both had the same purpose. Each used the pattern of Israel's past as a way to interpret the present. In the process, each portrayed Jesus as incomparably greater than any of the ancient heroes on whom his story was modeled. And this is because very early in the Church's life, companions of Jesus searched their scriptures in an effort to understand him and make sense of his fate. Already in these "overtures" we see how Christians used the Hebrew scriptures to interpret Jesus' significance. There are many more examples of this process in the gospels.

You're saying that Matthew and Luke tell different stories, yet both of them agree that he is born of a virgin. And you call these stories "religious fiction." Does that mean that you don't believe in the virgin birth?

It's true that both Matthew and Luke agree on the virginal conception of Jesus. But that story is a perfect illustration of the point I have been making about how some Christians searched their scriptures to find ways to speak about the significance of Jesus.

In Matthew's story that searching becomes quite explicit. When an angel speaks to Joseph about the son who is to be born to Mary, Matthew specifically

adds that "all this took place to fulfill what had been
spoken by the Lord through the prophet: 'Look, a virgin shall conceive and bear a son, and they shall name
him Emmanuel (which means God is with us.)'"

Look for a moment at the original setting of the
prophet's words, which are found in Isaiah 7:14. Over
seven hundred years before the time of Jesus, King
Ahaz of Judah, threatened by outside forces, was
encouraged by Isaiah to put his trust in God. When
Ahaz refused to be assured of God's assistance, Isaiah
prophesied a message of doom. But his prophecy had
nothing whatever to do with conception by a virgin.
The word in Hebrew is "*almah*," which refers to a
young woman just married but not yet pregnant with
her first child. Isaiah says that a young woman is soon
to conceive and bear a son; and before that child grows
to maturity, the attacking kingdoms and that of Ahaz
will lie devastated. God will indeed be Emmanuel, that
is, "God with us," but in judgment, not salvation.
Isaiah's prophecy was specifically addressed to people of
his own time. Matthew, however, read those ancient
words as a prophecy of hope rather than judgment, and
he took the term "virgin" to apply not only to the pre-
married state of the young woman, but to her state
even during and after conception.

Unlike Matthew, Luke does not specifically refer
to Isaiah's prophecy, though his language is so close to
that of Matthew that we must assume he had it in
mind.

What is going on? The passage in Isaiah was not a
prediction of Jesus, but a message to a king in Isaiah's
day. However, by the time the gospels were written,

Christians had already been searching their scriptures for any light they might throw on the identity of Jesus. They had already decided that Jesus was God's chosen one. He already had "saving power" for them. They already believed in the significance of the Jesus who had taught and healed among them and then been crucified. What they then did was *to project that faith in him backwards* onto the time of his conception and birth. Not *all* Christians did so, however. Since this story cannot be found anywhere outside the tradition used by Matthew and Luke, we know that not all Christians read the Isaiah passage in the same way.

By the way, when opponents of Christianity heard claims that he had been born of a virgin, they made the obvious rebuttal that he must have been born illegitimately. A pagan philosopher named Celsus, writing near the end of the second century, claims that the illegitimate father was a Roman soldier named Panthera. In that name we perhaps hear a mocking allusion to the word "*parthenos*," the Greek word for the young Hebrew "*almah*" from Isaiah 7:14.

So you're saying that the virgin birth story was not a fulfillment of prophecy, but a fiction based on an ancient prophecy.

Yes. Isaiah did not *predict* Jesus, but Christians did see in Jesus a *fulfillment* of their own prophetic history, and so they had no trouble using ancient traditions as the core of stories about him.

Let me be very clear. I interpret the story of a virginal

conception to be *a confession of faith about the significance of Jesus, not a biological statement about Mary's body.* The virgin birth is a symbol of faith in the adult Jesus, projected backward in time onto Jesus as an infant.

The same process was at work in the story of Jesus' birth in Bethlehem.

Both Matthew and Luke agree that Jesus was born in Bethlehem, a village that lies south of Jerusalem in the hills of Judea. But here again we are in the realm not of history, but of religious fiction, and for the same reason. Matthew specifically tells us that Jesus' birth fulfills an ancient prophecy in the book of Micah that a ruler of Israel would come out of Bethlehem. Though Luke does not quote the passage (Micah 5:2) explicitly, he also sees Jesus as the fulfillment of the hope for a messiah who would come from the line of David.

An interesting sidelight is that Matthew assumes that Mary and Joseph had been already living in Bethlehem. Luke, however, starts his story with Joseph and Mary living in Nazareth, and so he has to get them to Bethlehem for the birth. The way he does that is by his famous story about a decree

> *that went out from Emperor Augustus that all the world should be registered. This was the first registration that was taken while Quirinius was governor of Syria. All went to their own towns to be registered. Joseph also went from the town of Nazareth in Galilee to Judea, to the city of David called Bethlehem, because he was descended from the house and family of David. (Luke 2:1–7)*

However, there are several problems with that story. First, there never was a worldwide census under the Emperor Augustus. Second, though there was indeed a local census when Quirinius was governor of Syria, it came about ten years *after* the death of Herod the Great—who was supposedly still ruling when Jesus was born. Third, we know from taxation decrees in the Roman world that people were usually registered where they were living and working. They did not go back to their ancestral homes for registration and then return to their present homes for work. That would have been then, as today, a bureaucratic nightmare. It is a little sad to say this, because the story of the trip to Bethlehem and the birth in a manger is so beautiful and has inspired such a flowering of Western art, music, and devotion. But the reality is that the journey for census and tax registration is sacred fiction, a creation of Luke's imagination in order to get Jesus' parents to Bethlehem for his birth. Interestingly, in the Gospel of John, Chapter 7, we find an argument about whether or not Jesus is the Messiah, and some are arguing that he cannot possibly be since the Messiah must come from Bethlehem. Either the author of John had never heard a claim of a Bethlehem birth for Jesus, or, if he had, he didn't believe it.

All this may seem like nit-picking, and in a way it is. What really matters is that beneath these stories lies the conviction that Jesus was God's son and the Davidic Messiah. That expression of Jesus' significance is deeply embedded within all early Christian traditions. But these particular birth stories were known only to some Christian communities and are picturesque ways of expressing the common faith. In these stories, ancient scriptures are the engine that push the story line along.

So is there nothing in the realm of historical fact that we know about the birth and infancy of Jesus?

That would be overstating it a bit. Jesus was probably born a few years before the start of the first century, around the time of the end of Herod the Great's rule. He was born to Joseph and Mary at Nazareth, a tiny hamlet whose population was probably no more than a few hundred people. From Mark 6:3, we know that he had four brothers (James, Joses, Judas, and Simon) and at least two sisters (unnamed). And we know something about the social class into which Jesus was born—a subject which I will return to in the next chapter.

But the significance of the birth stories does not really lie in the historical data that they give us. The meaning of these stories lies elsewhere. Let me try to get at that meaning by telling you another story of a birth in that ancient Mediterranean world.

The Roman historian Suetonius tells this story of the conception of Augustus, Rome's first emperor and its ruler at the time Jesus was born. He only tells it, by the way, at the end of Augustus' biography, along with the marvels and signs that accompanied his death. On the night of his conception, Augustus' mother, Atia, fell asleep in the Temple of Apollo and was impregnated by the god in the form of a snake. Meanwhile, back at home, Augustus' father, Octavius, dreamt that the sun was arising from his wife's womb. Augustus, in other words, was conceived of a divine father and a human mother. And if you think that such stories had no political or social implications but were just imperial propaganda, look at this ancient decree of calendar change in the Roman province of Asia. It is found on marble stelae in all the Asian temples dedicated to Rome and Augustus.

> *Whereas Providence ... has ... adorned our lives with the highest good: Augustus ... and has in her beneficence granted us and those who will come after us [a Savior] who has made war to cease and who shall put everything in [peaceful] order ... with the result that the birthday of our God signalled the beginning of Good News for the world because of him ... therefore ...*

and it goes on to decree that the new year shall begin for all the Asian cities on the birthday of Caesar Augustus.

In light of that decree, listen to Luke's story of the angel announcing Jesus' birth. For the moment do not even ask whether or not it is factual. Don't worry about whether or not it happened. Listen to it in the light of the proclamation about Caesar's birthday.

> *And she gave birth to her firstborn son and wrapped him in bands of cloth, and laid him in a manger,*

because there was no place for them in the inn. In
that region there were shepherds living in the fields,
keeping watch over their flock by night. Then an
angel of the Lord stood before them, and the glory of
the Lord shone around them, and they were terrified.
But the angel said to them, "Don't be afraid; for
see—I am bringing you good news *of great joy for*
all the people: *to you is born this day in the city of*
David a Savior, who is the Messiah, the Lord. This
will be a sign for you: you will find a child wrapped
in bands of cloth and lying in a manger." And sud-
denly there was with the angel a multitude of the
heavenly host, praising God and saying, "Glory to
God in the highest heaven, and on earth peace
among those whom he favors!" (Luke 2:7–14)

Now we begin to catch a glimpse of the real question posed by Luke and Matthew. Where is God to be
found on earth? In Augustus the emperor, or in Jesus
the peasant? Take both stories factually and historically or both stories metaphorically and symbolically,
but face their challenge in either case: where do you
find your God—with the powerful, the conqueror, and
the oppressor; or the powerless, the conquered, and
the oppressed?

To show that I'm not just imagining this question
from a twentieth-century point of view, let me go back
to the pagan critic, Celsus. He never argued that the
virgin birth was incredible, only that it was incredible
for a member of the lower classes—a Jewish peasant
nobody like Jesus. "What absurdity!" said Celsus. He
knew many stories of the divine births of Greek

heroes. His question of Jesus was: "What have you done by word or deed that is quite so wonderful as those heroes of old?" What bothered Celsus was not the claim that Jesus was *divine*, but the claim that *Jesus* was divine. In fact, class snobbery is very close to the root of his objection to Christianity. He complains that the religion of Jesus took root in the lower classes and spread mainly among the vulgar and the illiterate. So it is not just that Dominic Crossan, a twentieth-century scholar, says that the meaning of these stories lies elsewhere than in their literal understanding. The ancient critic also knew that the question was deeper than that, namely, whether or not in a lower class peasant nobody like Jesus, God could be revealed. Who could believe that?

Let me add that I think if we had Matthew and Luke here today and asked them whether we should read these stories literally, they would say, "But don't you see? You're missing the point!" So it is not enough to say there was no guiding star, no Wise Men, no manger, no Bethlehem, no shepherds, no angels, no virgin birth. All of those negatives are perfectly true, but they are also quite besides the point. They beg the real question, which was then, as now: where do you find the divine revealed on earth—in Caesar or in Jesus? In imperial grandeur or in peasant poverty? In domination and subjugation of others from the top down, or in the empowerment and liberation of others from the bottom up? Those are the questions of Christmas. And those are the questions that get us to the true meaning of the birth stories about Jesus.

If the virginal conception of Jesus is not literally true, are you saying that Jesus is not the Son of God?

Not at all. But I distinguish emphatically between a statement of fact and a statement of faith. To say that Jesus was human or that Jesus came from Nazareth is a statement of fact, which anyone can make. To say that Jesus is divine or that Jesus came from God is a statement of faith, which only Christians can make. That faith declares that we find God present to us especially, particularly, and uniquely in Jesus. But, Jesus as divine or Jesus as God-for-us is about our relationship to Jesus. It is not as if an electronic scan of Jesus' body would reveal anything different from normal human processes. Neither would his genes or chromosomes show anything inhuman or superhuman. The term "divine" asserts a relationship between God, Jesus, and believers.

In answering that last question, did you deliberately avoid using the title Son of God?

Yes, I think so. When the term "son" was emphasized in Jesus' world, it usually referred to the first-born son, and first-born son meant heir. We who call Jesus "Son of God" declare that all divine gifts come to us in and through Jesus. But in our present world, much father/son language appears chauvinistic and exclusive and I do not find it necessary to use it against that contemporary background. But I insist,

once again, that to confess Jesus as Son of God has
nothing to do with divine interference in Jesus' normal conception from Mary and Joseph. Virginal conception by divine intervention is a parable expressing
in fictional narrative what was already believed,
namely, the unique relationship between God, Jesus,
and Christian believers.

*Christianity has always claimed that it is
uniquely true because our Jesus was conceived
literally and historically by special divine intervention. What happens to that claim if Jesus was
not literally and historically conceived of the
Virgin Mary by the power of the Holy Spirit?*

All faith, like all love, must be experienced as radically particular and absolutely unique. When a man
loves a woman, *this* man loves *that* woman. Our
humanity is, at its deepest moments and profoundest
depths, particular. Imagine this: I wake up tomorrow
morning next to my wife and say, "If I had not met
you, fallen in love with you, and married you, I would
probably have met someone else, fallen in love with
her, married her, and be waking up next to her this
morning." That is a very imprudent way to start one's
day, and yet we know that it is quite true. But once
again, our humanity is achieved in particularity. So
faith, like love, must be experienced as unique, absolute, irreplaceable. But we must also know that others
experience their faith as equally unique, absolute, and
irreplaceable. Every religion, Christianity like all others,

must be experienced as absolutely unique to the
believer. But all religions, Christianity like all others,
must acknowledge that others experience that same
uniqueness. Religions may and even should compare
themselves with one another in public discourse, but
no religion can claim an initial monopoly on the holy,
the sacred, or the divine. Indeed, in any such monop-
olistic claim there lies embedded a genocidal impulse.
One way I alone can be absolutely right is for all others to be dead. And one way for all others to be dead is
for me, us, or our God to kill them. The challenge for
the next millennium is to hold on to one's own faith
with total integrity without having at the same time
to negate or destroy that of others.

3

What Does John the Baptist Have to Do with Jesus?

I'm a religious [nun] for over forty years! . . . In this time of my life, I find that the church has betrayed me! These wonderful things the biblical scholars are discovering/recovering about Jesus and the early church are things we should share and be revitalized by. I feel so alone and have no one to share the Eucharist with. [It] seems meaningless unless we celebrate community. But going to church on Sundays and other days just frustrates me. . . . Is the bread we eat the Body of Christ or is it symbolic of his presence? . . . To be honest, it does not make too much difference to me. What is happening is so important. Symbol can become a reality.

A woman from Michigan

My own experience leads me to believe that Crossan plays no intentionally radical role, but rather has moved to the only place his increasing archeologi-

cal, anthropological, sociological knowledge will allow
him to dwell with integrity. . . . Mystery need not be
irrational. There is enough Mystery in the fact . . .
that Christianity still lingers though its leader was so
swiftly dealt with. And there is Mystery enough if
Jesus' message of a radically egalitarian society, with
no mediator necessary between anyone and God,
should tenaciously survive, long enough for archeol-
ogy, anthropology, sociology and believers like
Crossan to lift the veil and beckon us to see the Light
of that message still shining.

A woman from Michigan

Thank you for your work with the Jesus Seminar
and for your individual work on the life of Jesus. As
I have been reading your books my faith has become
deeper and more real. You and your colleagues have
said things that I have always known deep in my
heart. . . . Reading your work has helped me come
to a deeper commitment in my faith, and to rededi-
cate my life to teaching adults within the church. I
had abandoned this Call ten years ago for personal
and institutional reasons, but the model of faithful
ministry that you present has given me the courage to
re-evaluate that decision.

A woman from Michigan

I'm just a poor half-illiterate security guard who
happens to believe that the Bible is the infallible
Word of God. . . . My question to you, Dr.
Crossan, is who appointed you as the heir to
Jehoiakim? Who chose you to intellectually cut and

burn the Gospel of God? Don't you see how you're hurting God's faithful?

A man from Alabama

I think you're on target. . . . If the work of the Jesus Seminar is not buried, and (so to speak) "Jesus speaks plainly once more"—then there are going to be some whollopping changes in this old world! There could be inflammatory response—like the Ayatollah's to Rushdie. There could be incredible malaise . . . you and the rest making about as much splash as a story in The National Inquirer—or perhaps there might be a new reformation! Who knows.

A man from South Carolina

Some time ago I listened to an interview with you on Station WBAY, The Idea Network of Wisconsin. . . . I was somewhat dismayed by your comments on Jesus and John the Baptist. (1) John did not put himself above Jesus; (2) John the Baptist said, "I must decrease, and you increase." (3) He is universally known as the forerunner of Jesus. . . . I noticed the interviewer excellently raised questions against your diminishment of Jesus Christ.

A woman from Wisconsin

For Jesus to have changed his view of John's mission and message at that time in the history of the Jews, in that place, would have confused his followers and destroyed his credibility. Only a

*Gentile, past or present could accept either the
views of Christianity or your views. Few Jews, past
or present could accept either position. Whatever
you feel or believe about me, I believe you to be a
courageous and worthwhile human being.*

                                        A man from Florida

*Regarding the Baptizer—here in the Q
Gospel—he seems to be a desert (hermitic) cynic-
sage. Could it be that the Christians apocalyptacized
him as they did Jesus? This does not undo Jesus' distinctiveness, but rather sees it in the difference
between hermit and wayfarer.*

                                  A man from South Carolina

**What about those details in Luke regarding the
circumcision and presentation of Jesus in the
Temple, about the prophecies of Anna and
Simeon, and especially about that scene in the
Temple when Jesus was twelve years old?**

Recall what I mentioned earlier about Luke's parallel infancy stories in which Jesus is consistently
exalted over John the Baptist. The stories mentioned
in the question are part of that process. Jesus, of
course, would have been circumcised, as were all
male children of observant Jewish parents. But John
the Baptist, for example, was presented to the world
in the restricted space of his own home, whereas
Jesus was presented to the world in the Temple itself.

But it is especially that incident at twelve years of age that exalts Jesus far above John the Baptist, since the latter has no comparable story. That account of Jesus' precocious brilliance is very similar to what Josephus tells us about himself in his autobiography. When he was "a mere boy, about fourteen years old," he was so learned "that the chief priest and the leading men of the city used constantly to come to me for precise information on some particular in our ordinances" (*Life* 9). Those stories about Jesus or Josephus are standard assertions of moral and Biblical excellence. Neither of them offers factual details, but rather fictional ways of expressing a child's future importance by having it appear already in infancy or early adulthood.

It seems to me I remember an advertisement for a book about "the hidden years of Jesus." How much do we know about his childhood?

Really, nothing at all, in terms of history.

From time to time books are written that purport to tell long-lost stories of Jesus' childhood and youth. These are based on legends that never found their way into the New Testament. Pious imagination couldn't rest content with the restrained interlude of Luke, "And the child grew big and strong and full of wisdom, and God's favor was upon him." And so a fabric of legend was woven to wrap around the child Jesus. A second-century infancy gospel, for example, tells how when he was five years old Jesus took some soft clay and made twelve clay sparrows. A neighbor, who was offended because this broke the rule against working on the Sabbath, complained to Joseph, who rebuked his son. At this Jesus responded by clapping his hands and saying, "Off with you!" and the clay sparrows came to life and flew chirping away.

In such stories, the supernatural child was not always so cute and innocent in using his powers. We are told that when he got angry he cursed and withered those who got in his way, so that Joseph once commanded Mary, "Do not let him go outside the door, for all those who provoke him die." Not one of these legends, of course, has even a kernel of historical truth in it. The reality is that about Jesus' childhood and youth we know nothing. In itself that is not at all surprising. As so often happens in the early years of one famous only much later, nobody was watching or caring at that earlier period. Caesar Augustus, Roman emperor at the birth of Jesus, opened his official autobiography with the words "At the age of nineteen," thereby ignoring everything that had happened before that crucial adult moment.

When you talked about the birth stories, you mentioned that we know something about the social class into which Jesus was born. That must mean that we know something about his childhood.

That's true.

What we know about Jesus' social class comes from the same source that tells us about his brothers and sisters. In Mark 6:3 we read, "Is not this the *carpenter*, the son of Mary and brother of James, Joses, Judas, and Simon, and are not his sisters here with us?" That tells us not only that Jesus had four brothers, but what their names were, and that he had at least two sisters. It tells us more by identifying him as a carpenter. By the way, when Matthew tells the same story, he changes the question of the villagers to, "Is not this the carpenter's *son*?" So the tradition tells us that either Joseph or Jesus, or perhaps both (in a society where sons often followed in their fathers' footsteps), were carpenters. So the question is: what does that tell us about the social class into which Jesus was born?

It is important to avoid interpreting the word "carpenter" in modern terms. Nowadays a carpenter is a skilled, well-paid, respected member of the middle class. That wasn't true in the first century. The Greek word translated here as "carpenter" is "*tekton.*" One scholar of the Greco-Roman world has published a "lexicon of snobbery" filled with words used by literate upper class writers that show their prejudice against illiterate lower class people. "*Tekton*" is one of those words of disdain.

The Greco-Roman world was sharply divided between those who had to work with their hands and those who did not. On the upper class side of that chasm were four groups: the *governing class*, who made up one to two percent of the population but owned fifty percent of the land; the *priests*, who might have owned as much as fifteen percent of the land; the *retainers*, bureaucrats and army personnel

who served the governing and priestly classes; and
the *merchants*, who probably began in the lower
classes but might have ended up with substantial
wealth and even political power. On the lower class
side of the chasm were, first, the *peasants*—the vast
majority of the population, about two-thirds of
whose crop went to support the upper classes. They
lived at a bare subsistence level, and if drought or
debt or disease or death forced them off their land,
they ended up as sharecroppers, tenant farmers, or
worse. Next came the *artisans*, about five percent of
the population, who were lower than the peasants in
social class because they were usually recruited from
the ranks of dispossessed peasants. Finally, beneath
the artisans, came *degraded and expendable classes*—
who either had occupations that made them outcast,
or were reduced to begging, day labor, outlawry, or
slavery.

If Jesus was from a carpenter family, he belonged
to the artisan class. That meant that he was lower
than peasantry, one of those pushed into the dangerous space between peasants and the degradeds or
expendables. He was, therefore, living on the edge of
mere subsistence. And since at the time of Jesus
between ninety-five and ninety-seven percent of the
Jewish state was illiterate, we must assume that Jesus
also was illiterate. Like most of his contemporaries in
an oral culture, he would have known the basic stories of his tradition, but not the exact texts or argu-
ments of the learned scribes. That tells us, for
example, that the scene in Luke 4, where his adult
skill in interpreting a passage in Isaiah astonishes his

fellow villagers in Nazareth, is an invention of the gospel writer. What Luke does—as a literate skilled interpreter of scripture himself—is to rephrase the spoken challenge and charisma of Jesus in terms of scribal literacy and interpretation.

So, historically, we first meet Jesus as a man from lower class origins who goes with many others to be baptized by John in the Jordan River.

How sure are we that Jesus was baptized by John in the River Jordan?

Nothing is more certain about Jesus than this: that he was baptized by John in the Jordan River.

The reason for our certainty is that the Christian tradition shows increasing embarrassment about that baptism. Wherever we find the Church embarrassed by a tradition about Jesus, the odds are very strong that the tradition is rooted in actual history. And why was the Church embarrassed by the story of Jesus' baptism? Because it would seem to say that Jesus, like others, underwent baptism "for the forgiveness of sins," and because it seems to put John in a superior position as the one who baptized him.

So although Mark tells the baptism story without any defensive commentary, he immediately adds to it the story of a heavenly voice coming to Jesus saying, "You are my Son, the Beloved, with you I am well pleased." Matthew goes much further by having John protest to Jesus, "I need to be baptized by you, and do

you come to me?" Finally, in the Gospel of John,
John the Baptist witnesses to Jesus as the Son of God
without any account of an actual baptism. By then
the baptism of Jesus by John is gone and only the
revelation about Jesus' significance remains. This
whole process of development shows us that
Christian communities were uneasy about suggesting
that Jesus might have needed baptism for the forgiveness of sins or be in some way subordinate to John.
Since the Church would hardly have invented a
story that caused it such problems, that very embarrassment gives us confidence in the historical reality
of the baptism.

*When I think of John the Baptist, the first thing
that comes to my mind is that gruesome story of a
dancing girl asking for his head to be delivered
to her on a platter. Why did John come to such an
abrupt, violent end?*

The biblical story that you refer to (found in Mark
6:17–29) tells how Herod Antipas sent men to arrest
John because he had criticized Herod for marrying his
brother Philip's wife. The irate woman in question
then had her daughter, who danced before the king,
reply to his offer to reward her by asking for John's
head—a request which the king, having made a
solemn vow, could not refuse. That is a marvelously
dramatic story, but it is fiction. In fact, it's probably
derived from an earlier and well-known Mediterranean
horror story about a Roman senator in the preceding

century who was expelled from office because he had a prisoner beheaded at a banquet to satisfy the curiosity of his mistress. In other words, it was a traditional story about how *not* to exercise power.

What, then, was the historical reason for the arrest and execution of John?

The first-century Jewish historian, Josephus, had this to say about the ministry of John the Baptist:

> *When others, too, joined the crowds about him, because they were aroused to the highest degree by his sermons, Herod became alarmed. Eloquence that had so great an effect on mankind might lead to some form of sedition, for it looked as if they would be guided by John in everything that they did. Herod decided, therefore, that it would be much better to strike first and be rid of him before his work led to an uprising, than to wait for an upheaval. . . . John, because of Herod's suspicions, was brought in chains to Machaerus . . . and there put to death.*

Notice what we are told here: that John aroused people by his sermons, that many were willing to follow him in all that they did, and that the authorities feared that it might lead to some form of sedition, or even to an uprising. Obviously, John was seen as posing a threat much more serious than merely commenting on the marital arrangements of Herod Antipas.

Take a look at what the *Q Gospel* says about the content of those sermons of John that so aroused people (Matthew 3:7–12):

> *You offspring of vipers! Who warned you to flee from the coming fury? Change your ways if you have changed your mind. Don't say, "We have Abraham as our father." I am telling you, God can raise up children for Abraham from these stones. Even now the ax is aimed at the root of the trees. Every tree that does not bear good fruit is cut down and thrown into the fire. . . . I am plunging you in water; but one who is stronger than I is coming, one whose sandals I am not worthy to touch. He will overwhelm you with holy spirit and fire. His winnowing fork is in his hand to clear his threshing floor and gather the wheat into his granary. The chaff he will burn with a fire that no one can put out.*

What does this mean? John was talking about a God who was going to come very soon as an avenger. God is like a forester with an ax separating good trees from bad ones, like a thresher separating grain from chaff. In John's fiery vision there are just two ways, the good and the bad, and the time is short for people to decide for one side or the other. Like ancient prophets he announces that God is coming to set right an evil situation and to save an oppressed people. John is, in other words, an apocalyptic preacher announcing the coming of an avenging God.

An "apocalyptic preacher"? What does "apocalyptic" mean?

"Apocalyptic" is a word that takes us to the very heart of my argument about John—and indeed Jesus. So we need to take some time to get clear about it. But first, let me sketch in a bit of historical background.

Down to the present day we often talk about the *Pax Romana*— the Roman Peace. We have, in other words, accepted Rome's self-understanding as expressed in the famous lines of Virgil's *Aeneid:*

Roman, remember by your strength to rule
   Earth's peoples—for your arts are to be these:
   To pacify, to impose the rule of law,
To spare the conquered, battle down the proud.

That is a very benign view of Roman power and rule. But think for a moment what that rule looked like and felt like from below—from the viewpoint of the conquered ones.

The Roman historian Tacitus wrote a biography of his father-in-law, Agricola, who governed Britain in the late first century. In that biography he has a rebel general describe the Roman Empire from his point of view: "To plunder, butcher, steal, these things they misname empire: they make a desolation and they call it peace."

That is the view of the *Pax Romana* from the underside. And so the question becomes: how do oppressed people react when they have been conquered militarily, overwhelmed economically, beaten

down socially? There are two ways. One way is to
fight again and again, usually losing against overwhelming power. In the first century there were a
number of such Jewish uprisings against Roman
power—often sparked by *messianic leaders*, so called
because they were thought to be "anointed" by God
to restore the kingdom promised to David and his
successors. Often these messianic leaders expected
supernatural assistance—in the style of their remembered traditions. A second response is that of *apocalyptic prophets*. These do not look for a military
rebellion by human beings, but announce that God's
own power is soon going to accomplish what human
resistance cannot accomplish, namely, a total victory
of good over evil and the arrival of a world of justice
and goodness.

The latter is what I mean by "apocalypticism." It
is waiting for God's action to end intolerable oppression and evil and bring a new, just, and perfect world
into being. And what I am arguing is that John the
Baptist was the first in a series of apocalyptic
prophets who appeared in the Jewish homeland until
it was destroyed in the late 60s for rebellion against
Rome.

So there were others preaching in the style of John the Baptist?

From both Josephus and the New Testament we
know that there were a number of leaders who took
throngs of people out into the desert, promising to

show them signs of God's forthcoming deliverance.
And here it's very important to see the significance
of going out into the desert and recrossing the
Jordan. Remember that Moses and Joshua in ancient
times led the Israelites through a time of desert wandering and into the Promised Land. What these
apocalyptic prophets were doing was taking people
back into the wilderness, crossing the Jordan, and
reentering the Promised Land as their ancestors had
done with God's assistance. We're even told that
one such prophet announced that at his command
the walls of Jerusalem would fall down. That
reminds us of Joshua marching around the walls of
Jericho waiting for a spectacular victory from God.
The apocalyptic prophets thus hoped to do by divine
power what they could not do by mere human
strength.

That is why John gathered people for baptism at
the Jordan River.

*But John never led people in a mass movement
against the regime, did he? All he did was bap-
tize individuals.*

True. John was *like* the other apocalyptic prophets
in that he announced and awaited God's intervention
to set right the oppressions and evils of the present
day. But John was *unlike* many other apocalyptic
prophets in that he did not gather followers together
to lead them *en masse* into the Promised Land. John's
strategy seems to have been different. When people

came to him, he kept sending them back from the
wilderness, through the Jordan, purified and forgiven
into the Promised Land, there to await the imminent
coming of the avenging, saving God. In essence, John
was forming a giant system of purified individuals—a
network of ticking time bombs all over the Jewish
homeland. Because of John, when Jesus began his
ministry, he found already a vast network of people
expectant, eager, waiting for God's power to be
revealed.

So Jesus began as a disciple of John?

Jesus was certainly baptized by John in the Jordan
River. Like many others, Jesus was part of a ritual
reenacting of the Moses and Joshua stories of the con-
quest of the Promised Land by God's power. So Jesus
became part of that network within the Jewish homeland of people waiting for God's coming. What were
they waiting for? Presumably for God to do what they
lacked power to do—destroy Roman power. Jesus
began as an apocalyptic believer. He began in the tradition of John.

We have ample evidence in gospel stories of Jesus'
high opinion of John. In the Q Gospel (Matthew
11:7–9 or Luke 7:24–26) Jesus speaks of John as not
only a prophet but "much more than a prophet." He
also says (Matthew 11:11 or Luke 7:28) that "no one
born of a woman is greater than John; yet the least in
God's kingdom is greater than he." In those last words
we are introduced to a *separation* between Jesus and

John. Jesus has regarded John as not only a prophetic figure, but as greater than the prophets. Yet at the same time he now announces that the least in the Kingdom of God is greater than John. What does this mean?

I want to return later to that phrase the "Kingdom of God," but for now I'll simply say that Jesus makes a distinction between John as the culmination of the past and the newly arrived Kingdom of God which holds the future. Something new is happening, Jesus is saying. It belongs not to John in the desert, but to the child in the Kingdom. What this means is that *Jesus has changed his view* about John's mission and message. For Jesus it is no longer enough simply to await God's intervention to bring in a new world. One must enter a new world—which he calls the Kingdom— *here and now*. The Kingdom is an ever-present reality in which Jesus lived and into which he invited all whom he met to enter. Perhaps it was John's execution that led Jesus to understand that God did not and would not change the world through imminent apocalyptic restoration. Jesus would begin to move in a new direction: It is not that we are waiting for God, but that God is waiting for us.

But Jesus does seem to be an apocalyptic figure— at least as the gospel writers portray him. What are we to make of sayings like "The Son of Man will come on the clouds of heaven"?

The question about the "Son of Man" sayings has been one of the most hotly debated in New

Testament studies. My conclusion is simply this: That while New Testament writers attribute the title "Son of Man" to Jesus—clearly meaning an apocalyptic deliverer who is to come—Jesus did not refer to himself by such a title. Jesus used "son of man" in a generic sense, simply to mean (and this was the original meaning of the phrase) *human being*. But apocalyptic use of the phrase "Son of Man" with respect to Jesus was a tradition that grew up about Jesus after his death.

There are many different ways in which a radical challenge can be thrown down to present worldly powers. *Ascetics* withdraw from the world into caves, deserts, or monasteries. *Nihilists* try to destroy the world with words, deeds, or bombs. *Apocalyptic prophets* announce that the world is so evil and beyond human remedy that only immediate divine intervention can set it straight. *Jesus comes with a different strategy.* He challenges the present structures of life through the creation of a new kind of community which here and now embodies the values of "God's Kingdom."

The difference between John and Jesus is made crystal clear in a segment of the *Q Gospel* (Matthew 11:18–19 or Luke 7:33–34):

> *John did not come eating and drinking, and they are saying, "He is demon possessed." The son of man [that is, Jesus] has come eating and drinking, and they say, "Look at him, a glutton and a drunkard, a friend of tax collectors and sinners."*

The contrast is between a *fasting* John and a *feasting* Jesus. John lives an ascetic life, alone, out in the desert. Jesus gathers people around a dinner table, building a new kind of human community. In chapters to come I will say more about what that means. What we have established so far is what John was, how Jesus began, and how eventually, in his own words and in the eyes of others, Jesus became something very different from John—indeed, almost the exact opposite of the Baptist. Jesus certainly challenges the world in which he lives, but in a very different way from the apocalyptic prophet who announces the imminent judgment of God.

I have read that John the Baptist lived for a time at Qumran among the Essenes. Is that accurate?

Most people have heard by now of the Dead Sea Scrolls. These are manuscripts, some complete, but the vast majority in fragments, discovered in caves along the northwestern shore of the Dead Sea in the Jewish homeland. It is generally held that the Essenes, dissident priests who had broken with the official Temple priesthood about a century and a half before the time of Jesus, lived in the enclave now called Qumran and buried their library in the caves before the attack of the Romans in the first Jewish revolt of 66–74. Those Essenes had withdrawn into the desert, but west of the Jordan, unlike John to the east; and they awaited the arrival of twin Messiahs, one priestly and one lay, unlike John who awaited the arrival of

God without any mention of a preceding Messiah (before, of course, the Christian gospels had adopted John the Baptist as the forerunner of Jesus). John's once-and-for-all baptism, by crossing from the desert through the Jordan River into the Promised Land, is totally different from the daily purification rituals at Qumran. I see John's movement, therefore, as quite distinct from that of Qumran, oriented toward the general populace rather than an educated group living in isolated community.

4

What Did Jesus Teach?

Congratulations on compromising and denigrating the beautiful thing we call "faith" and reducing it to your empirical and media-centered "scientific" search for the TRUTH! . . . I am not some religious extremist and do not belong to a televised "group" or anything. I am simply a father and husband struggling to make my own contribution in this life and support a higher sense of morality and values within my family life. . . . Please review what you are doing and I pray that you stop this harmful process and affront to the very One that gave us His Son for our salvation.

A man from Texas

Rarely if ever have we read anything quite so revolutionary, quite so liberating and so deeply challenging as your book. I have long since stopped thinking of Jesus as God (i.e. the Trinitarian ontology) although the metaphor of God-dying-in-Jesus allows some very challenging images. But I clung to an ontology of resurrection (a la Paul). Your book has shown me that even that is not necessary to be a follower of Jesus and confess Jesus as Lord.

A couple from South Africa

Prof. Crossan seems to suffer from selective reading of the Bible. . . . Jesus clearly champions the poor, sick and oppressed. He clearly tries to change the hearts of people to care and share for them. . . . Crossan ignores the portrayal that Jesus has rich friends without telling them to give all they have to the poor as he did the rich young lawyer. The obvious lesson is that Jesus felt that differences in living standards were acceptable providing that one is responsible in one's use of one's talents and resources by substantially aiding the poor and oppressed. Communal living did not last very long even amongst those committed early Christians.

A man from California

[In] thirty years of pastoral work, it just has not been possible to keep up with the intense debate which has obviously framed so much of your own work. During my time [at seminary] pastoral concerns were at the top of the list. I found that epilogue [to Who Killed Jesus?] to be one of the most refreshing perspectives on faith and scholarship and commitment I have read in a very long time. This letter is intended to simply thank you for strongly presented scholarship. I may or may not agree with your conclusions; it will take some time to decipher much of what I find. But I am very grateful that you took time in this particular

debate to be personal and encouraging to others
who work as pastors.

A man from Texas

Professor Crossan, I say this in Christian love
and care for your life in eternity, that you recon-
sider just who Jesus really is and that HE lives even
right now at the Right Hand of God the Father,
interceding for you and all who have believed on
Him— as Saviour and Lord—Coming Bridegroom
and King of Kings and Lord of Lords—May the
Lord help you to see, in Christ's love,

A man from Alabama

Where I'm coming from right now is to accept
the historical findings—and begin to reflect on these
sayings, individually and in small groups and try to
perform them in our lives.

A man from Arizona

I was very unhappy with your position on a
revised mission for Jesus and your concept of the Son
of Man, Kingdom of God and how to achieve it. I
felt that things I had come to believe about Jesus
were being attacked and decided to defend, I have
never done this before. . . . It is reasonable for me to
think that Jesus believed in the imminent ending of
the world and in his return in splendor before this
generation passed away. I believe that Jesus was like
John. They both preached for people to repent and
that the Kingdom of God was at hand.

A man from Florida

I am now re-reading the book [Jesus: A Revolutionary Biography] in order to answer a few questions I have. . . . Could you define the God you said is "available to you (and all of us)"? My second question would be . . . define the Kingdom of God. My feeling is that it is here and now at the table described in the parable where we all sit down and eat together without any class, religious, ethnic or economic lines or distinctions among us.

A man from New Hampshire

You usually hear that Jesus taught about the Kingdom of God. Is that right and what does it mean?

We have an immediate problem with that phrase "Kingdom of God." Matthew, for example, prefers to avoid the name of God out of reverence for its holiness, so he usually rephrases that expression as the "Kingdom of Heaven." We tend to hear that as the "Kingdom *in* Heaven," as if Jesus was talking not about earth, but about heaven; not about this life, but about the next life. Nothing could be farther from the truth. And to understand Jesus' meaning we must not separate religion and politics, ethics and economics in that first-century world. "Kingdom of God" means what this world would look like if God, not Caesar, sat on its imperial throne; if God, not Caesar, was openly, clearly, and completely in charge. It is, at the same time, an absolutely religious and absolutely political concept. It is absolutely moral and absolutely economic at the same time. How would God run the world? How does God want this world run? It is not about heaven, but about earth.

As we have already seen, for one group of people in the Jewish homeland—apocalypticists, like John the Baptist—the Kingdom of God was understood as a *future* reality. Not only was it future, but it depended on the *overpowering intervention of God* in human affairs to bring justice and peace to an earth felt to be almost hopelessly mired in injustice and oppression. At the very most, the faithful could prepare for or assist the arrival of the Kingdom, but its accomplishment would come by God's power alone. And although apocalyptists were serenely vague about the details of that coming Kingdom, they were clear that it would be objective and visible to all— but with appropriately different fates for the good and bad.

There was, however, another way of thinking about the Kingdom of God. Instead of us waiting for God to begin an apocalyptic intervention, God is waiting for us to begin a social revolution. It is, in both uses, the Kingdom *of God*, because neither solution is deemed possible by simple human endeavor. But a divine apocalyptic intervention is very different from a divine social revolution; and Jesus, having abandoned John the Baptist's hope for the former, turned instead to announce the latter.

Why continue to use an expression like "Kingdom of God"? Why not replace it with, say, the "Community of God"? That is surely more appropriate than anything with an exclusively male word like "king" in it.

For several reasons that word "kingdom" poses some problems as the translation of the New Testament Greek word *"basileia."* For one thing, the "king-" part of the word is chauvinistic. For another, the "-dom" part of the word makes it sound as though we're talking about some locality, some piece of geography. And a third problem is that in our contemporary world we have no real sense of what it meant to be ruled by monarchs. To be sure, we watch with fascination the pomp and ceremony that surround the few remaining crowned heads in the world—like Queen Elizabeth II of England—yet we all recognize that her role is traditional and ceremonial, but not powerful.

In the Mediterranean world into which Jesus was born, however, the king had power indeed. And it was not only Jewish apocalyptic prophets who were concerned about *basileia*—kingly rule—in the first century. *Basileia* was a common subject in the Hellenistic world, and the issue was this: how should power be exercised in a just and humane way? The gospels are wrestling with the contrast between how *human* power and *divine* power are exercised. When Jesus uses a phrase like the "Kingdom of God," he is talking about *what the world would look like if God were directly and immediately in charge.* What would the world be like if God sat on Caesar's throne? The Kingdom of God is a symbol for an ideal description of human life, transcending and calling into question all existing forms of human rule and social order. A term other than "kingdom" might lack that political-religious challenge.

Members of the Jesus Seminar proposed translating the Greek word as "God's imperial rule" to emphasize the contrast with Caesar's imperial rule. It is that critical social edge and subversive political tone that I try to maintain by holding on to "kingdom" rather than "community." Were I to use that latter term, I would lose Jesus' political-religious challenge: whose is the kingdom, the power, and the glory? God's or Caesar's? But, by all means, use "community" instead of "kingdom" as long as the subversive social challenge and critical political edge are present in the meaning.

An example might help. Imagine a German Christian community in the early 1930s that called Jesus *"der Führer"* and insisted that there was only one such *Führer*. In itself that is a very ordinary German word meaning "leader"; yet, after Hitler's advent, that Christian usage clearly would have meant: Jesus is our leader, Hitler is not.

Use, therefore, any modern translation you want for "Kingdom of God," but remember that it should always have overtones of high treason. Similarly, to say that Jesus was Lord meant that Caesar was not. Translate "Lord" with any contemporary expression you deem appropriate, as long as it is one that could get you killed.

Are you saying that the Kingdom movement was just promoting a worldly, political reform?

No. Let me introduce a very important scholarly adjective: "eschatological." It comes from a Greek word meaning "about the end of this world," and it can be applied properly to either divine apocalyptic intervention or divine social revolution. Recall that situation just discussed, when one believes the world has become seriously and profoundly evil and therefore needs serious redemption. Such profound redemption might be termed "radical," "ideal," "utopian," "counter-cultural," or "eschatological." All those words indicate an ending of this present normal world and its replacement by a perfect alternative. A divine apocalyptic intervention or a divine social revolution are two alternative scenarios for such an ideal, utopian, or eschatological solution. The former is the message of John's Baptism movement. The latter is the message of Jesus' Kingdom movement.

When Jesus was teaching did his followers record his words about the Kingdom of God as they were spoken?

Jesus, we must always remember, was not a literate, upper class scribe, but an illiterate peasant. He spoke with an oral brilliance that few academically trained persons ever attain. Whenever we read words ascribed to him that were written down by literate classes decades and even generations after his death, we must recognize that his first audiences would have retained only the most striking images, the most startling analogies, the most forceful plot summaries of stories that might have taken hours or more to tell.

*I want to turn now to some practical conse-
quences that Jesus draws from his teaching concerning the Kingdom of God. Why does he attack
so fiercely what we might term "family values"?*

In twentieth-century America the supreme value is probably *individualism*, but the supreme value of the first century might rather be called "*groupism*." That value was based on kinship and gender relationships. What we find in Jesus are some biting sayings about Mediterranean family values. Here are three examples.

The first example is from Mark 3:31–35:

> *Then his mother and his brothers came; and standing
> outside, they sent to him and called him. . . . And he
> replied, "Who are my mother and my brothers?" And
> looking at those who sat around him, he said, "Here
> are my mother and my brothers! Whoever does the
> will of God is my brother and sister and mother."*

Jesus makes an almost savage attack on family values as they were understood in the Mediterranean world—and makes it more than once. Then, as now, the family was a group to which one was *assigned*. But in the text just quoted, Jesus downplays the family in favor of another kind of group that is *open to all who*

wish to join it. For Jesus, the given family unit, the kinship unit, is no longer primary. What is primary is a
new community of persons who become "family" to
one another in their common effort to do the will of
God in the world.

A second example is that of a woman in the
crowd around Jesus who blurted out a blessing upon
his mother: "How fortunate is the womb that bore
you, and the breasts that you sucked!" (Luke 11:27).
But in response Jesus turned back the compliment,
saying, "How fortunate, rather, are those who listen
to God's teaching and observe it!" The woman
declares that Mary is blessed because of Jesus. In typical Mediterranean fashion, she believes that a
woman's greatness derives from being the mother of a
famous son. Though it's a common attitude in a patri-
archal society, Jesus will have none of it. What he
offers is a blessedness that is open to anyone who
wants it, without distinction of sex or gender, infertility or maternity.

A final example is from the Q *Gospel*, in Luke
12:51–53:

> *"Do you think that I have come to bring peace to the
> earth? No, I tell you, but rather division! From now
> on five in one household will be divided, three against
> two and two against three; they will be divided:
> father against son and son against father, mother
> against daughter and daughter against mother,
> mother-in-law against her daughter-in-law and
> daughter-in-law against mother-in-law."*

The usual interpretation of this passage is that families will become divided as some believe in Jesus and others refuse to put their faith in him. But I think the point has nothing to do with family *faith*, but with family *power*. Notice that the dividing line in the parable is between the generations. Jesus pictures a typical Mediterranean family with five members, mother and father, unmarried daughter, married son and his wife, all living under one roof. Jesus says he will tear it apart. His attack is on the Mediterranean family's power arrangement, which has father and mother in authority over son, daughter, and daughter-in-law.

This story, in fact, helps us to understand all of Jesus' stories and teachings about family life. The family is society in miniature, the setting in which we learn patterns of love, hate, helping, abusing. Not all families are Norman Rockwell scenes of warmth and nurturing. Since family life involves power, it also invites the abuse of power, and that is the point of Jesus' critique. His ideal group is contrary to customary human social arrangements, a group that is open and equally accessible to all under God. In the Kingdom of God there is no abuse of power. All are welcome, all are equal, and all are alike under the will and purpose of God.

Even in our twentieth-century democratic society, far removed from the authority patterns of Jesus' world, we have become painfully aware of abuses of power in family life. The phrase "domestic violence" is heard much more than it was a generation ago. We now know that gross abuses of power often lurk behind the facade of domestic tranquillity. So whether in the first century or the twentieth, Jesus' critique has something to say: No given structure of family life is absolute; all structures exist for human nurturing. Family life, like all human life, comes under the critique of the Kingdom of God. Family life, like other forms of human association, exists for purposes of justice and love.

The sayings of Jesus about society seem just as radical or even as negative as those about the family. Why is that?

I use just one example here, but it is a very radical saying of Jesus that takes us deeper into his sense of the Kingdom. This saying is found in four different versions. Luke's version is: "Blessed are you who are poor, for yours is the kingdom of God" (Luke 6:20). What we see in the other versions is how uncomfortable the tradition became with that saying in its stark form and how hard interpreters worked to soften it.

For example, when Matthew records the phrase, it becomes: "Blessed are the *poor in spirit*, for theirs is the Kingdom of heaven" (Matthew 5:3). Matthew changes "poor" to refer not to the economically destitute but to the religiously humble, thus blunting the force of Jesus' word. Moreover, in the letter of James, the poor are called "rich in faith and heirs of the kingdom which he has promised" (James 2:5). The Kingdom is now no longer a present reality, but a promised future, and the poor are those who are *rich in faith.* Both Matthew and James have filed away the rough edges of a saying linking the poverty-stricken and the Kingdom.

Moreover, we have a very serious problem when the Greek word in the gospel text is translated as "poor." That word really means "destitute." The Greek language has a separate word for "poor," which describes a peasant family that makes a bare subsistence living from year to year. But the actual Greek word used in the beatitude refers to a family that has been pushed by disease or debt or drought or death off the land and into destitution and begging. The *poor* person has to work hard but has enough to survive, while the *destitute* person has nothing at all. In other words, Jesus did not simply declare the poor blessed— a class that for all practical purposes included the entire peasantry—but declared the destitute and the beggars blessed.

Well, what on earth does that mean? Did Jesus really think that beggars were specially blessed by God—as if all the destitute were nice people and all the upper class were evil?

I don't think this saying reflects a naive or romantic illusion about how charming it is to be destitute. I do think that it is important to hear this, not just in an individual sense, but in a social sense. That is, Jesus and his fellow peasants found themselves in a structured system of injustice. In situations of oppression, especially where injustice is so built in to the system

that it seems normal or even necessary, the only ones
who are innocent or blessed are those who have been
squeezed out deliberately as human junk from the
operations of the system. If Jesus were to speak this
message among us today, it might come out like this:
"Only the homeless are innocent." And that is, of
course, a terrifying saying. It is terrifying because, like
his words against the family, it focuses not just on
individual abuse of power but on abuse in its systemic
forms. Such sayings cut because while we may feel
innocent of *personal* wrongdoing, as participants in
social systems that are unjust, none of us has clean
hands or a clear conscience.

The most important conclusion from that saying is
that the Kingdom of God is a critique of systemic
rather than just individual evil. It not only says, as it
were, do not rape or brutalize your slave, but claims
that slavery is against the radical justice or absolute
equality demanded by God. Jesus' criticism is systemic
and structural rather than individual and personal.

So far we have been speaking of the sayings or
aphorisms of Jesus, but what about his stories or
parables? Is not Jesus, above all, a teller of tales,
a speaker of parables?

If you read any of Jesus' parables today it takes you
less than a minute to do so in most cases. But those
versions are only plot summaries. An actual telling or,
better, acting of a parable might have taken Jesus an
hour or so and must have involved frequent audience

interaction to agree or disagree, comment on or discuss. In such a situation, Jesus' parables would have been scenes of debate not just about religion or theology but about politics and economics. They would have steadily raised audience consciousness about the systemic injustice of imperial rule and colonialism. They would have drawn regular attention to the divergent fates of aristocrats and peasants and to that terrible line between poverty and destitution. When you read a parable, think of the divergent responses, probably loud and immediate, from different classes or genders within a common audience. A parable empowers rather than dominates an audience. It challenges them to think and judge for themselves. It is the most appropriate teaching technique for a Kingdom of God in which God empowers rather than dominates, challenges rather than controls.

But what would that have to do with, say, the parable of the mustard seed which simply says that the Kingdom starts out very small but ends up great and large?

That's a common interpretation. But we need to take a look at Mediterranean mustard plants—and also at nesting birds. It's true that mustard plants do start as proverbially small seeds and grow into shrubs that are three or four feet high, or even higher. But I really don't think that we have yet got to the real point of Jesus' parable.

Pliny the Elder, who died in the year 79 when he

approached too close to the erupting Mount Vesuvius, wrote about the mustard plant in his book *Natural History*. He described its pungent taste and "fiery effect"—which he thought was very beneficial to the health. He noted that the plant grows entirely wild, although it can be improved when transplanted, and added, "When it has once been sown, it is scarcely possible to get the place free of it, as the seed when it falls germinates at once." In other words, he is saying that the mustard plant tends to take over where it is not wanted, that it tends to get out of control, and that it is difficult to eradicate. Jesus claimed that this new Kingdom of God is like a pungent shrub with dangerous takeover properties. In fact, in cultivated areas it tends to attract birds where they are not wanted—no farmer likes to have them around eating up his seeds and grains. Again, this is a startling metaphor: the Kingdom is a pest to those who own carefully cultivated gardens. Do you think landowners, tenant farmers, day laborers, unemployed workers, or destitute beggars would all respond alike to that startling image of the Kingdom of God as a mustard plant?

So parables were more than just "sermon illustrations"? They forced people to make decisions about their meaning?

Take a look at a parable of Jesus which helps answer that question affirmatively. In fact, it helps us understand all those other sayings about the Kingdom of God to which we have so far referred. It is found in several different versions; I am quoting from the Gospel of Thomas 64.

> Jesus said, "A person was receiving guests. When he had prepared the dinner, he sent his servant to invite the guests. The servant went to the first and said to that one, 'My master invites you.' That person said, 'Some merchants owe me money; they are coming to me tonight. I must go and give them instructions. Please excuse me from dinner.' The servant went to another and said to that one, 'My master has invited you.' That person said to the servant, 'I have bought a house and I have been called away for a day. I shall have no time.' The servant went to another and said to that one, 'My master invites you.' That person said to the servant, 'My friend is to be married and I am to arrange the banquet. I shall not be able to come. Please excuse me from dinner.' The servant went to another and said to that one, 'My master invites you.' That person said to the servant, 'I have bought an estate and I am going to collect the rent. I shall not be able to come. Please excuse me.' The servant returned and said to his master, 'The people whom you invited to dinner have asked to be excused.' The master said to his servant, 'Go out on the streets and bring back whomever you find to have dinner.' Buyers and merchants [will] not enter the places of my father."

The final sentence, "Buyers and merchants will not enter the places of my father," is Thomas's interpretation of the parable's meaning. When Luke tells the story, he mentions "outcasts" who are called into the meal, and Matthew mentions "good and bad" who are gathered. But behind all those separate interpretations we can see a common story line.

Jesus tells a story about a person who prepares a dinner party and sends out his servant to invite friends to attend. Each one of the persons invited has an excuse for being unable to come. So here is a dinner ready, but a room empty. And so the host sends his servant to replace the absent guests with anyone he can find off the streets.

Think about that situation for a minute. If anyone had been brought in off the street, there undoubtedly would have been sexes, classes, ranks all mixed up together. Anyone could have been reclining next to anyone else: female next to male, free next to slave, socially high next to socially low, ritually pure next to ritually impure. And that, of course, would have been a social nightmare and a threat to all the carefully constructed conventions of social life in the first century.

Well, not only in the first century. Can you seriously imagine someone in the present day throwing a dinner party and just inviting anybody who happened to be wandering down the street?

Exactly the point. Think for a moment of a beggar coming to your door. Maybe you would give that beggar some food to take with him on the road. But would you invite him into your kitchen for a meal, or bring him into the dining room to have supper with your family, or have him come back Saturday night for a supper with a group of your friends? Or again, suppose you were the CEO in a large company. Think of the difference between holding a cocktail party in the office for all employees, a lunch at the restaurant for middle managers, or a private dinner party for your vice-presidents at home. In the twentieth century, as in the first century, who we invite to eat with us in what sort of situation says a great deal about social standing and relationships.

So eating is not simply a physiological act to get rid of hunger pangs. Anthropologists tell us that *the "rules" of eating are miniature models of a society's rules about people's relationships and behavior.* What we do at the dinner table serves as a map of economic, social, and political differences.

To take a twentieth-century example, think back to the United States at the start of the civil rights movement. Think of the furor that erupted at a Woolworth lunch counter when black young people sat there to order a sandwich or a Coke. This modern, enlightened, democratic society had rules about who could eat and drink where, when, and with whom. It was literally against the law for blacks to eat in certain places, and certainly for blacks and whites to eat together. That segregated lunch counter was a miniature model of the patterns of association in the segregated society as a whole. So when young people, black and white, broke the rules and sat around tables together to eat (or rode in the same bus), they were creating a new model of what the society should look

like. The *segregated table* symbolized human separation
and discrimination; the *open table* symbolized human
community, oneness, equality. And that is exactly
what was going on in the ministry of Jesus.

But a parable is just a story, isn't it? Who would ever take it literally?

It was only a story, of course, but it was a very
pointed story that challenged the society's miniature
model, the table, as a place of hierarchy and separation. And it was really more than a parable because
Jesus lived out his parable by calling around his table
people of different genders, social classes, and religious
scruples. Do you remember that accusation mentioned
earlier that John the Baptist was possessed because he
fasted, and that Jesus was a glutton and drunkard
because he ate with sinners, tax collectors, and even
whores. That, of course, is but nasty name-calling in
both cases, but even name-calling must have a logic,
must have some basis in fact to be valuable as invec-
tive. Jesus' *living out* that parable of the open table is
what produced the accusation that he was a glutton
and drunkard, a friend of tax collectors and sinners.
The critics were saying, in other words, that he made
no appropriate distinctions and discriminations. And
since *women* were present when he was at table, especially unmarried women, the obvious accusation
would be that "Jesus eats with whores"—"whore"
being the standard insult directed at any female who
was outside socially approved male control. So all of

those terms—tax collectors, sinners, whores—are derogatory terms for those with whom, in the opinion of the name-callers, open and free association should be avoided.

So for Jesus, the Kingdom of God is pictured as a new kind of meal arrangement. A nondiscriminating table depicts in miniature a nondiscriminating society, and this vision clashed fundamentally with the basic values of ancient Mediterranean culture. It is not too soon to suggest that one can see, in the outrage that followed Jesus' new habits of table association, the reason for the arrest and execution that would later bring his ministry to its end.

Where does the Last Supper fit into this picture?

Our sense of that meal has been colored, of course, by the ritual traditions of our churches, whether called "Communion," "the Lord's Supper," or "the Eucharist." Jesus may well have had a last meal with his disciples, but the historical question is whether he instituted a new Passover meal, symbolizing his martyrdom, with the instruction to repeat it in his memory. The evidence is mixed. Paul certainly knows about such an institution (1 Corinthians 11:23–25). But the *Didache*, a late-first-century document, describes a communal eating custom among Christians and shows no awareness of a ritual deriving from the Last Supper, no connection with the Passover meal, and no commemoration of the death of Jesus. So I would put the situation this way: What Jesus left behind was the tradition of open eating as a sign of the inclusiveness and equality of life in the Kingdom of God. Later, c e r tain Christian groups created the Last Supper ritual, adding a commemoration of Jesus' death to that tradition of shared meals.

You referred earlier to the civil rights movement in the U.S. as an illustration of Jesus' movement in the first century. Isn't there a problem here that when you speak about the openness and equality between people that Jesus was modeling, you are painting a picture with contemporary colors? Aren't you just projecting modern democratic values backward into the first century?

No, I am picturing something much more radical than our experience of contemporary democracy.

Let me put it this way. Those who, like peasants, live with the boot on their neck have a choice between two different dreams. One dream is of a world in which they in turn can put their boots on those other necks. That is the quite understandable hope or even plan of *revenge*. But an alternative dream is of *justice*—a world in which there would never again be any boots on any necks. Consider, for example, these words of an unnamed peasant woman from Sicily, speaking to a northern Italian journalist during a peasant uprising in 1893:

> *We want everybody to work, as we work. There should no longer be either rich or poor. All should have bread*

*for themselves and for their children. We should all be
equal. I have five small children and only one little
room, where we have to eat and sleep and do everything, while so many lords have ten or twelve rooms,
entire palaces. . . . It will be enough to put all in
common and to share with justice what is produced.*

There were in the first century plenty of people in
the Jewish homeland who looked toward a future of
revenge. Jesus was among the ones who envisioned
instead a future of justice. The open table, the end of
abusive power, the radical equality that is expressed
in Jesus' sayings, and modelings of the Kingdom of
God are not simply a prefiguring of modern democracy. They are more radical, more terrifying than anything that we have ever imagined. And even if we
can never fulfill, or even accept that vision, we
should not try to explain it away as something less.
We should avoid doing what even the gospel writers
frequently did, namely, taming the words and deeds of
Jesus to make them easier to understand and to do.
The vision of the Kingdom of God that Jesus offered
may not be immediately translatable into every real
human social situation. Its relevance is that, as vision,
it always exists in creative tension with every social
situation and all customary human arrangements—
hopefully, spurring us to greater efforts to remove
abuses and to embody justice. It announces a God of
radical justice who calls us to establish nothing less
than that on earth. If we reply that such is not possible, God might respond that, in the long run then,
neither is the world.

Was Jesus' message about the Kingdom of God all talk or did it involve action as well? Did Jesus offer an idea or a program?

We have already seen that Jesus lived in a time of social turmoil, and that a phrase like the "Kingdom of God" had social and political meanings for those who heard it. It was, one could say, one hundred percent religious but also one hundred percent political, one hundred percent theological but one hundred percent social and economic as well. Is it possible that Jesus' teaching was merely *spiritual* and not related to the crisis his people were facing? Why, in any event, would oppressed peasants listen to him? It is a particular temptation for those of us who are scholars or preachers to interpret Jesus in purely intellectual terms as a part of the history of ideas. But what I want to insist upon here is that Jesus not only *discussed* the Kingdom of God, but *acted it out* and invited others to act it out as well. If, in fact, all he had done was talk about the Kingdom, lower Galilee would probably have greeted him with a great big peasant yawn.

I have argued that it was Jesus' active practice of inviting people to a common table in violation of the customary social norms that brought about those nasty accusations that he was "a glutton and drunkard, a friend of tax collectors and sinners." His open table was intended as a miniature model for society. I want to insist that the same thing was happening with the *healings* of Jesus. They are not simply individual acts of compassion, but are another way of modeling the Kingdom of God in opposition to the established patterns of society's life. If we are not to reduce Jesus to a teacher of abstract ideas alone, it is crucially important for us to understand his free healing as well as his open table. And that points us into the next chapter.

5

Did Jesus Perform Miracles?

[In Haiti] I have seen a little girl try to ease her hunger
by eating dirt. When I approached her, she covered her
lips to conceal the mouthful of grit and pebbles, but
tiny telltale stones glistened on her lips and chin. . . . I
feel so stirred and inspired by Crossan's description of
Jesus as a radical egalitarian who broke down barriers
to celebrate table fellowship with all manner of people.
I just wish we could set a table for the little Haitian boy
who cried in my arms last night. . . . I asked him why
he looked so sad. He burst into tears, eyes full of pain,
and whispered, "I'm hungry."

An American woman in Haiti

I have just finished reading your book and thank
you for writing it. After a while I will have to read it
again to understand much of it. It is very interesting
but does not go into many things that bother me. All
my life I have had difficulty with the concept of God,
and have been working on it. What did Jesus say
about God?

A woman from Puerto Rico

Thanks to your books, I am now in the process of "un-doing" thirty years of "doing theology and calling it history and doing Christian apologetics and calling it academic scholarship." If I were only fifty years younger, you would find my name on your class lists. . . . Thanks a million for making my old age more exciting.

A man from Florida

There are still secrets and mysteries to be revealed. But the Bible says there is nothing hidden that will not be revealed. I doubt that it would be revealed to a professor of religion at DePaul University. Most likely to the woman who cleans the rooms or the janitor who unplugs the sinks . . . I really wonder if . . . you found Jesus? I know you would try to hide it but I can tell you now, you'll never be successful. I thank God for giving me this opportunity to write you.

A woman from Illinois

I attended a seminary for three years and also have consulted many people, and the more one lives the more one sees and understands there is more to life than just bold scientifically provable or demonstrable things—there is also an eternal spiritual world all around us that can in the person of Jesus or a saint or someone else today . . . break into time and actually heal—our little time warped minds should not try to limit or deny divinity—so Jesus may also have actually healed or raised from the dead as well as accepted people sociologically back into the community.

A man from Illinois

I've been working at a VA hospital caring for stroke patients. . . . At night in my emergency room when I meet someone and just see the hurt and the need there, the supernatural, saving Christ image makes me sick, like some type of stupid joke. It's not that I don't believe that the Christian hope voiced in the language of myth, particularly the confession that suffering can be healed, cannot sometimes become real. Personally, I believe that hope for the redemption of our world lies in the extent to which we can share emotional, spiritual, social, and physical healing. The question is not whether suffering can be healed, but how do we induce this healing? How do we help each other become whole? I want to find out.

A woman from Missouri

With all due respect, I would like to suggest that there may be more taking place in those healing stories than you seem to allow: There may have been real healing of the disease, to borrow a term you use, not just a healing of the illness. . . . Almost all of the healings attributed to Jesus in the canonical Gospels involve what could have been psychosomatic symptoms.

A man from Minnesota

[The possessed woman in the "Overture" to The Historical Jesus: The Life of a Mediterranean Jewish Peasant *had what is*] called "clinical depression"—nothing more, nothing less—the most "un" and "mis" diagnosed ailment

on our big blue ball. Was it actually around for
your basic first-century peasant Jew? Trust me, in
big supply. . . . Now just imagine Jesus "itinerat-
ing" right across some major boundaries. . . . He
passes out the best "healing" that ever was and ever
will be—KINDNESS. No big deal huh? Actually, it is
still the only universal "treatment.". . . I still say if
Jesus [cured in a] trance, how on earth could he ask
the rest of us to go and do likewise without giving
lessons? Was he asking "all" the others to go do just
what he did—or something "kind of" like he did or
what? If it factors down to anything less—you've
screwed yourself—I say.

A woman from South Carolina

**What about those nature miracles? For example,
did Jesus walk on the water or did he not? Did
Jesus create a miraculous catch of fishes or did he
not?**

There is one striking difference between the
nature miracles and the healings or exorcisms of
Jesus. The nature miracles are performed for the disciples (or mother) of Jesus but the healings or exorcisms are for outsiders. Even the multiplication of
loaves and fishes is performed through the disciples,
who act as intermediaries in requesting, serving, and
clearing the meal. In the two cases mentioned, those
miracles are not for ordinary people, but for the official followers of Jesus. Why? Think of the stories

once more. The disciples row on the Lake of Galilee
without Jesus and get nowhere against the storm.
Jesus comes to them walking on the waters; all is
immediately safe and well. The disciples fish on the
Lake of Galilee without Jesus and catch nothing.
Jesus calls to them from the shore; they catch more
than they can handle. I consider those twin stories
to be clearly symbolic: without Jesus nothing, with
Jesus everything. In the boat of the Church it is
Jesus who counts and Jesus who is in charge. The
disciples even as leaders are totally dependent on
Jesus.

*But did those who originally wrote those stories
intend them to be read literally?*

I do not think so. It is not that ancient people
told silly stories which we, because we are so smart,
should not take literally or factually but symbolically
or fictionally. It is the ancients who knew how to
tell a good metaphorical story (a parable, if you prefer) and we moderns who are silly enough to take
them factually.

I have, of course, not gone into all the so-called
nature miracles, but that preceding answer tells you
how to generalize about them. The nature miracles
are authority parables. They are not about Jesus'
power over nature, but about the disciples' authority
in the Church. Sorry if that is disappointing, but I
insist that to take them literally is to misread them
completely.

You made a distinction earlier between nature miracles and human miracles such as Jesus' healings or exorcisms. What about them?

The healings and exorcisms come from a very different viewpoint and they concern outsiders or strangers rather than the insiders or disciples. But allow me a moment of autobiography because my general understanding of God's presence in human history is important here.

I have visited Lourdes in France and Fatima in Portugal, healing shrines of the Christian Virgin Mary. I have also visited Epidaurus in Greece and Pergamum in Turkey, healing shrines of the pagan god Asklepios. The miraculous healings recorded in both places were remarkably the same. There are, for example, many crutches hanging in the grotto of Lourdes, mute witness to those who arrived lame and left whole. There are, however, no prosthetic limbs among them, no witnesses to paraplegics whose lost limbs were restored. What do I conclude?

Faith heals! That is as sure as anything we can ever know. Certain diseases for certain people under certain circumstances can be healed by faith in that very possibility—at Epidaurus for a pagan, at Lourdes for a Christian, at Benares for a Hindu, and so on. But certain diseases only, certain people only, and certain conditions only. And that is exactly what Jesus said again and again: Your faith has healed you. I do not understand that process completely (nor does anyone else) but, leaving aside fakes and charlatans, faith heals—sometimes. Did people come to Jesus to be healed? Absolutely. Were some or even many healed? Absolutely. But there had to be something about Jesus that made people come to him for healing as distinct, say, from John the Baptist to whom they went for baptizing, not healing. That is the question we should probe. Of course certain people were and are healed by their *faith* in Jesus, but why was it faith *in Jesus*?

Can you give me a concrete example of how Jesus healed somebody?

Remember the story of the leper. I use it as a case study of what we have been discussing.

First of all, it is important to note that the modern term "leprosy" is flatly wrong as a translation of the Greek word used in this story. That Greek word actually referred to several different skin diseases, all of which involved a rather repulsive scaly or flaking skin condition—such as psoriasis, eczema, or fungus infections. So whenever the Bible uses the word "leprosy," it must be understood as referring to those diseases rather than to what we now call "Hansen's disease" or "leprosy."

I don't mean to be rude, but who cares what the ancient disease was? Isn't it really the healing that counts?

Yes and no. Of course the healing of an individual sufferer matters. But what we have in this story goes deeper than that; it is an enacted parable about the society as a whole.

You remember what we were saying earlier: that the table is a miniature model of relationships within the society as a whole. The same thing is true of the individual human body. Anthropologists tell us that *the body is a symbol of the society*; the way one deals with the human body expresses an understanding of social relationships and differences. Every adolescent knows that tattooing arms, coloring hair, piercing anatomy, or adorning the body can either challenge one's group quite fundamentally, or affirm one's group connection. In the 1960s, for example, long hair immediately sent a message about one's attitude toward the established institutions of society. And you won't find dreadlocks in a Marine boot camp. So, when we look at healing stories, we need to be alert to "body image" issues in Jesus' society.

Yes, but what does that have to do with these skin diseases that you say are mistranslated as "leprosy"?

These diseases exactly illustrate the point that the body becomes a symbol of the whole society. The Jewish state was a society always threatened with absorption by a more powerful and imperial culture. In such a situation of political, military, cultural, and religious oppression, an emphasis on protecting *social* boundaries was symbolized by an emphasis on protecting *bodily* boundaries. So our question is: When Jesus

heals the leper, is he acting only as a healer of disease
or also as a critic of society?

It sounds pretty far-fetched to me.

I don't deny that in these stories we are entering a
world of thought and practice that is very, very strange
to us. That may, indeed, be the beginning of wisdom:
to recognize that the world of the biblical story is, in
many ways, not our world. That recognition will at
least keep us from making gross errors of assuming that
we can understand it on twentieth-century terms.

But let me suggest that the sense of the individual
body as a model for the body politic is not so far-
fetched after all. I mentioned that a threatened society, like the Jewish state, has an intense interest in
establishing and protecting boundaries. One of the
ways that this shows up in the law book called
Leviticus is in numerous rules about the body's openings—about food going into the body, or babies coming out of it. The problem of these diseases lumped
together as *leprosy* is that they cause openings to
appear on the skin where they are not meant to be—
in other words, all the boundaries are broken, and the
bodily system breaks down. (In Leviticus, by the way,
leprosy applies not only to skin, but also to clothes
and to house walls.) Each surface is in some circumstances made ritually unclean—that is, socially inap-
propriate. I realize that this is a very strange way of
thinking to the modern mind, but it does help us to
see that the person with a skin disease—the "leper"—

is a source of social concern, not simply because of medical contagion, as we might imagine, but because of *symbolic contamination*. The breakdown of the boundaries of the body symbolizes a threat to the integrity and security of the society as a whole. That's why in Leviticus 13:45–46 we read:

> *The person who has the leprous disease shall wear torn clothes and let the hair of his head be disheveled; and he shall cover his upper lip and cry out, "Unclean, unclean." He shall remain unclean as long as he has the disease; he is unclean. He shall live alone; his dwelling shall be outside the camp.*

That last line tells us what society's view of the afflicted individual was: "He shall live alone; his dwelling shall be outside the camp." What Jesus did was to welcome the outcast back inside the community from which he had been expelled. That *welcome home* was the healing.

I'm confused. Are you saying that the leper was really healed, or not?

I don't want you to think I'm evading all your tough questions, so let me just say: Yes, he was healed. That being said, bear with me a bit while I make a distinction between *curing a disease* and *healing an illness*.

Studies of many different societies have shown us that disease and illness are not the same thing. Doctors diagnose and treat *diseases*, but patients suffer *illnesses.* To put it bluntly, a disease is something between me, my doctor, and a bug. Something is wrong with my body, and I take it to a doctor to be fixed. And that's important. But there are other dimensions of my experience that are missing from that picture, not just the entire *psychological* meaning of the disease to me, but, much more important, the entire *social* dimension of it. How have I been brought up to think about my body, about modern medicine, about doctors? How does whatever is wrong with me affect my family, my job, or even wider levels of society? *Disease* sees the problem in a narrow, physical focus; *illness* sees it in a wider psychological and social context.

Think, for example, of AIDS. Did you see Tom Hanks's portrayal of an AIDS sufferer in *Philadelphia*? Was his suffering only what was going on in his body's immune system? Or was it also what he experienced in rejection, loss of his job, struggle to find a lawyer? There is a tremendous difference between curing the disease and healing the illness in AIDS. A cure for the disease is absolutely desirable, though not yet discovered; but where we cannot cure the disease, we can still heal the illness—by refusing to ostracize those who have it, by empathizing with their anguish, and by enveloping their suffering with respect and love. That is precisely what Jesus was doing with the leper—welcoming back into social relationship the person who had been an outcast. Jesus healed the illness, rather than the disease. If Jesus were here today, I do not for a moment believe that he could cure the disease known as AIDS, but I

am confident that he could heal the illness known by
that same name.

So you are saying that Jesus healed the leper, but it was not a miracle?

It all depends on what you mean by miracle. If you
mean the use of supernatural power to set aside the
usual workings of the natural world, then, no, it was
not a miracle. And it certainly was not—as is sometimes claimed—a proof of Jesus' divinity, since he told
his followers to do precisely the same thing. Jesus, in
my view, was not curing a disease through an intervention in the physical world, but was healing the illness through an intervention in the social world. He
healed by refusing to buy into the customary sanctions
against diseased persons. Jesus healed the "leper" by
inviting him back into human community, that ideal
human community called the Kingdom of God. He
refused to accept the disease as ritual uncleanness,
thereby forcing others either to accept the leper back
into the community or to reject Jesus from it as well.
The power of healing is a gift of God built permanently into the fabric of the universe, not just a tem-
porary or periodic intervention of God into a closed
universe which lacks such possibility.

There is one more aspect of the story that I ask you
to notice. In inviting the leper back into the community of God's people, Jesus was issuing a challenge to
those who were the society's boundary keepers. He
offered himself as an alternative boundary keeper in a

way that was quite rightly seen as subversive to the established procedures of his society. His *welcome home* to the leper put him on a direct collision course with the priestly authorities in the Temple who had charge of such boundary situations. Mark captured that original meaning in his closing comment, ascribed to Jesus, that the leper should go to the priest "as a testimony to them." That phrase might be better translated "as a witness against them"—in other words, "as a challenge to them." Perhaps it does seem to some that such an interpretation destroys the miracle. But I believe that miracles are not changes in the physical world so much as changes in the social world. It would, of course, be nice to have certain miracles available to change the physical world if we could, but it seems to me much more desirable to make certain changes which lie within our power in the social world.

If you have found it tough going to enter into the mental world of the healing of the leper, the going is about to get tougher still. We need also to deal with the fact that the historical Jesus is undeniably portrayed to us as an *exorcist*, casting out demons.

Jesus, an exorcist? Are we seriously to believe in demon possession, let alone that Jesus cast demons out?

Unquestionably, talk about *demons* and *unclean spirits* is weird to us. Let me say at the outset that I, myself, do not believe that there are personal, supernatural spirits who invade our bodies and, for either good or evil, jostle for control with our own personality. But the vast majority of the world's people have so believed, and according to one recent survey, about seventy-five percent of the human population still believes in such spirit possession. So we have to ask some difficult questions. What is it they are seeing, and why are they seeing it that way? Are we seeing something completely different, or the same phenomena through different eyes? I'm sure, in any case, that we haven't explained anything by simply saying, "I don't believe in demons." We may not have the same diagnosis, but that doesn't mean there are no symptoms to explain. On the other hand, it does make a difference what form of explanation we use. Let me illustrate that with two examples.

One psychiatrist tells the story of Mary, a thirteen-year-old girl on the Yakima Indian Reservation in central Washington. A local medical doctor had diagnosed her hysterical symptoms as paranoid schizophrenia and prescribed a potent drug. The psychiatrist, however, was sensitive to the girl's culture. He learned that her dying shaman grandfather had prophesied that his power would descend to her, but that she herself wanted to become a part of the majority American society. Since the psychological conflict was rooted in a sense of unwanted shamanistic spirits, he advised a native ceremony of exorcism. After that ceremony the girl recovered completely. In her culture of origin that ritual made sense and was therefore effective.

On the other hand, I recall an exorcism ritual that

was shown on prime time American television a few years ago. Those involved in the ritual all believed that the young girl was possessed, and when the priest came away from confronting the screaming, cursing patient, he announced that he had looked into the face of evil. But does the category of *demon possession* prove most fruitful for understanding that case? If, for example, some type of multiple personality disorder was hidden behind that supposed demon possession, the face of evil might be, in fact, sitting in the next room in the form of, say, an older male who had sexually abused the girl in infancy and shattered her unformed personality into defensive shreds. Calling her *demon possessed* implies blame for the victim, who must surely have done something to have caused such a fate. Would it not make more sense to use the contemporary diagnosis of multiple personality disorder, which involves no further victimizing of the victim? In other words, *names matter*. It may not make any sense at all to take categories of demon possession and exorcism into our contemporary world. But it makes a great deal of sense to ask what those words meant (and sometimes still mean) in other cultures.

Recall one of the biblical stories of exorcism. Mark (5:1–17) tells us that Jesus once came to the country of the Gerasenes. There he met a man with an *unclean spirit* who lived amongst the tombs, so powerful that no one could bind him, even with chains. He was always crying out and bruising himself with stones. When he saw Jesus, he yelled, "What have you to do with me, Jesus, Son of the Most High God? Do not torment me." Jesus asked him what at first may seem to be a strange question, "What is your name?" He answered, "My name is Legion; for we are many." Then we are told that the demons begged Jesus to send them out of the man into a herd of pigs feeding on the hillside, and Jesus gave them permission to go, after which about two thousand pigs rushed down a bank into the sea and were drowned. People from the surrounding countryside came to see what had happened, found the man who had been possessed by demons now calm, clothed, and in his right mind. And the story concludes, "They began to beg Jesus to depart from their neighborhood."

Let me be clear that I do not regard this as an actual scene from the life of the historical Jesus. Though Jesus' exorcisms are often mentioned in the gospels, we have no example of *particular stories* that are verified by more than one source. What seems to have happened is that the general tradition of Jesus as an exorcist eventually led to invented stories about what that ministry looked like. And so the question we need to ask about this particular story is: What do we see in it? What seems to be going on?

Well, for one thing I see a rather shocking indifference on Jesus' part to other people's property! Seriously, it just comes across to me as a bizarre story with no redeeming social significance.

It's strange, all right. But in light of the studies I mentioned earlier that show the individual body to be a symbol of the whole society, take a look at two of its features. First, when asked his name, the possessed man replies, "My name is *Legion*." The Legion, of course, is a unit of Roman military power and symbolizes the oppressive overlord of the Jewish homeland. That power is cast out into the most impure of Judaism's ritually unclean animals, and then (and this is the second feature I want you to notice) the Legion is *cast into the sea and drowned*. Who can possibly miss that most fervent dream of every Jewish freedom fighter—that the Romans be pushed back into the Mediterranean Sea?

There is a close connection between *possession* and *oppression*, whether the subjugation be the sexual one of women by men, or the racial and imperial one of some people by other people. An occupied country has, as it were, a multiple personality disorder. One part of it hates and despises the oppressor, but the other part envies and admires its superior power. And if the body is a symbol of the society, certain individuals may well experience exactly the same split within themselves. In the first-century mind, I am arguing, there was a connection between demonic possession and colonial oppression.

Isn't it possible that as a twentieth-century scholar you are simply reading back your understanding into first-century minds?

We always have to be careful that we do not simply retroject contemporary concerns into ancient minds, but let me give you an example that helps persuade me that it is not so in this case. The story concerns the Lunda-Luvale tribes of what used to be northern Rhodesia. According to one scholar they had traditional ailments resulting from possession by ancestral spirits that were called "*mahamba*." But then they developed a special modern affliction called "*bindele*," which is their word for "European." This new ailment required for its healing a special exorcistic church and a lengthy curative process. It seems to me that the *Legion* of Mark's story was to colonial Roman Palestine as *bindele* was to colonial European Rhodesia. In both cases colonial exploitation took on bodily form as demonic possession. When, therefore, Jesus exorcises, he is not simply healing individuals, but is engaging in symbolic revolution against the occupying power.

You haven't said much about how Jesus healed— in this case, how he "cast out demons."

It's a good question and, of course, extremely difficult to answer.

We know that in every culture are found altered states of consciousness and that these states are frequently used in healing. This is particularly true of premodern cultures with far less capacity to cure diseases than to heal illnesses. Native healers in many cultures have entered into trance states—altered states of consciousness—or produced such states in their patients as part of the healing process. In the modern world, physicians and psychologists use heightened

suggestibility in patients as part of the healing process—as is most clearly evidenced in hypnosis.

It is in this context that I want to take a brief look
at an incident where Jesus is attacked by his critics
(Luke 11:14–15):

> *Now he was casting out a demon that was dumb;
> when the demon had gone out, the dumb man spoke,
> and the people marveled. But some of them said, "He
> casts out demons by Beelzebul, the prince of demons."*

Beelzebul, the name of an ancient Canaanite god,
is here a symbol for Satan. You might again say that
we have here simply a case of name-calling. But as
with those accusations we mentioned earlier of glut-
tony and drunkenness, perhaps the name-calling is
based on something that makes the naming at least
possibly believable.

The question raised in my mind is whether Jesus
himself sometimes healed while in an altered state of
consciousness or trance. I am fully aware that there is
not much evidence for Jesus as an entranced healer
using contagious trance as a therapeutic technique.
But I am also aware that the talky, preachy, speechy
side of religion is also not too much at home with the
touchy, feely, squealy side. So it is at least possible that
the tradition ignored this side of Jesus even if it was
present there originally. I realize that my suggestion is
speculative, but I just want to leave the question open
for the future. This much is certain—and it is my bottom line—that Jesus not only *discussed* the Kingdom
of God, but *enacted it*, and that enacting meant heal-

ing people in a context that posed a challenge to both social authorities and imperial power.

Let me ask you a general question about miracles before we talk about Jesus. Do you believe in miracles then or now, ever or never?

Recall my earlier distinction between statements of fact and statements of faith. I apply it now to the distinction between marvel and miracle. A marvel is something for which I or we have no adequate explanation at the moment. And there are far more marvels around than we usually admit. I do not believe we live in a closed universe where we understand everything completely; and even if we understood the world completely, it would still be *our* understanding. So I expect to find multitudes of things I cannot understand or explain, what TV programs like to call mysteries and what I call marvels or wonders or puzzles. What is objectively present is a marvel, something we wonder about because we have no adequate explanation. When people declare that a marvel is a miracle, they are making an act of faith, they are declaring that, *for them*, God has acted directly and immediately in this situation, God has intervened outside normal, regular, or natural processes to create that marvel. That is, by definition, an act of faith, an ultimate interpretation beyond proof or disproof. There could not be an objective miracle unless we lived in an absolutely closed universe, all of whose processes and laws we understood. Then anything inexplicable would be a

miracle, an intrusion of the supernatural into the
closed system of the natural world.

But, granted that to declare a miracle is to make an act of faith, do you yourself believe in miracles?

Yes, but not as periodic intrusions in some closed
natural order. I leave absolutely open what God *could*
do, but I have very definite thoughts about what God
does do. The supernatural or divine is not something
that periodically or temporarily breaks through the normal surface of the natural or human world. The supernatural is more like the permanently hidden but
perpetually beating heart of the natural. It is always
there for those with spirit to see or faith to hear. And, if
every now and then, somebody sees an inbreaking presence here or there, I do not mock that claim because I
understand those experiences as subjectively read signs
of that abiding presence. What is seriously wrong for
me is to discern the holy only in the cracks and fissures
of the natural order rather than everywhere present
over, under, around, and through that natural order. I
believe, then, in miracles as the places where individuals or groups see God at work. Jesus is, for me, a miracle.

Is that a prejudice against miracles that invali-dates your reading of gospel claims about Jesus?

First of all, everyone draws a line of credibility
somewhere. Every time I stand at the grocery check

out I find myself confronted with weekly tabloids announcing gossip, scandal, and miracle. I do not believe any of them and if that's prejudice, so be it. Second, I presume natural consistency. When Aesop has animals talk I do not presume that animals spoke in ancient Greece nor that ancient Greeks believed they did. A standard presumption of natural consistency helps me identify the literary style of fable in which important moral lessons come disguised as talking animal tales. Aesop is a warning; if you take him literally you misunderstand him badly. I call that the "Aesop Fallacy" and it is far too prevalent in reading the Bible. Third, I also presume divine consistency: what God does now is what God always did. God "intervened" no more and no less in the world of the early first century than that of the late twentieth century. These are presuppositions or, if you prefer, prejudices, but so, of course, are the opposite opinions.

You said earlier that the healings of the pagan Greek god Asklepios and the Christian Virgin Mary are very similar to one another and to the miracles of Jesus. But what about those stories that Jesus raised people from the dead? What about Lazarus? Did those really happen?

It is interesting how densely the symbolic dimension surrounds a story like Lazarus. Here is a key section of the story:

Martha said to Jesus, "Lord, if you had been here, my
brother would not have died. And even now I know
that whatever you ask from God, God will give you."
Jesus said to her, "Your brother will rise again."
Martha said to him, "I know that he will rise again
in the resurrection at the last day." Jesus said to her,
"I am the resurrection and the life; he who believes in
me, though he die, yet shall he live, and whoever lives
and believes in me shall never die. Do you believe
this?" She said to him, "Yes, Lord; I believe that you
are the Christ, the Son of God, he who is coming into
the world." (John 11:21–27)

How shall we understand this story? In terms of
divine consistency, I do not think that anyone, anywhere, at any time, including Jesus, brings dead people
back to life. (I am not, of course, talking about near-
death experiences or about resuscitating apparent
corpses. Death means you don't come back. If you
come back, it was not death. Death, like pregnancy, is
either/or, not more or less.) But I think I can see what
is happening in this story, which in a very profound
sense is true.

To take an example from our own society, suppose
that you stood in front of a "Lincoln High School"
somewhere in Midwest America. And suppose that in
front of that school you saw a statue of Lincoln with
upraised ax ready to smash through the chains binding
a slave's feet. My question to you is: Is that true or
false? Well, of course, no such event ever happened,
yet that nonevent *symbolizes* the whole course and
meaning of Lincoln's life. Might we not say that the

symbolism involved in that statue is *true* even though no such event actually occurred?

That's what I think is going on in these stories of raising the dead. In John's gospel the event of Lazarus' restoration illustrates the general resurrection of the dead, an event in the distant future. But I can imagine peasants all over lower Galilee who would have said with equal intensity that Jesus brought life out of death for them right here and now in this present life. *Life out of death is how they would have understood their experience of the Kingdom of God* in which they began to take back control over their own bodies, their own hopes, and their own destinies. Jesus said that the Kingdom of God, the will of God for earth, was not Caesar's way; that it was diametrically opposed to Caesar's way; that it was the opposite of occupation and collaboration, oppression and domination, discrimination and marginalization. Such a claim was the first and most basic act of social healing, healing on the ideological level without which healing can never occur on any other level. His hearers who experienced the Kingdom of God's empowering presence knew that it meant life out of death; to have Jesus knock on the door of a tomb was an obvious parable for that experience. It was a dramatic video-bite, so to speak, for a much larger process.

My point, once again, is *not* that those ancient people told literal stories and we are now smart enough to take them symbolically, but that they told them symbolically and we are now dumb enough to take them literally. They knew what they were doing; we don't.

One final point connected with those healings.
Why does Jesus seem always on the move? As soon
as he heals somebody, he hurries off somewhere
else.

I think that picturing Jesus as always going somewhere rather than being settled in one place is thereby
interpreting what his ministry is about.

Let me get at this by noting an interesting problem
in New Testament study. We are told in Mark (6:4)
that Jesus' own family did not believe in him. Yet
when Paul arrived in Jerusalem, say, around the year
38, he found James, the *brother* of Jesus, already there,
along with Peter and in a position of authority. So we
have a problem. What happened in between? How did
James get from disbelief to belief and from Nazareth to
Jerusalem? What I suggest is that Jesus' family did, in
fact, believe in his power and mission but not at all in
the way he was carrying it out.

In Mediterranean culture, relationships were governed by patron/client ties. Remember that there was
a very small upper class and a very large lower class.
What kept society together were multiple ties
between patrons and clients. Those without power
could be clients to the patrons above them, and those
patrons might be clients to others far more powerful
still. Brokers were clients to those above them and
patrons to those below. The system, at its best, gave
some hope for recognition to lower class individuals
but, at its worst, confirmed their dependency and
oppression. I believe that the problem Jesus' family
had with him was that they wanted him to settle

down at his home in Nazareth and establish there a healing cult. He would be its *patron*, the family would be its *brokers*, and as his reputation went out along the peasant grapevine, the sick would come as *clients* to be healed. That would have been good for everyone. But instead Jesus kept to the road, brought healing to those who needed it, and, as it were, started anew every day. That was no way to run a healing ministry and no way to treat his family—especially in the world of Mediterranean values. So it's not surprising that once Jesus was gone, we find his brother James firmly settled, precisely located in Jerusalem—and in charge.

We have another story that throws light on why Jesus kept moving (Mark 1:35-38). He entered Peter's house, healed Peter's mother-in-law, and the town's sick people gathered for healing at Peter's door. Any Mediterranean person would know that Peter's house was becoming a brokerage place for Jesus' healing. But Jesus went out the next morning to a lonely place to pray, and when Peter caught up to him to take him back, Jesus said, "Let us go on to the next towns, that I may preach there also; for that is why I came out."

Mark created that story to show Jesus opposing Peter, because from Mark's point of view, they had different visions of mission. Peter was ready to have Jesus settle down and to broker his patronage to sick clients. Jesus was ready to move on because he offered an *unbrokered Kingdom* to all who needed him. The equal sharing of spiritual and material gifts, of miracle and table, cannot be centered in one place because that very hierarchy of place, of here above there, of

this place above other places, symbolically destroys
the radically open community it announces. For Jesus
the Kingdom of God is not his to offer as patron or
for others to broker. The Kingdom of God is a community of radical or unbrokered equality in which
individuals are in direct contact with one another
and with God, unmediated by any established brokers
and fixed locations.

6

Did Jesus Intend to Start a New Religion?

As an agnostic Jew, please know that I stand in awe
of the universe and the laws of nature. Where and
how it all started is surely beyond our present knowledge and maybe beyond any expectation of ever
knowing. Meanwhile, I suggest that human progress
will always be dependent on people like yourself who
are not beholden to rigid orthodoxy—and with the
courage to stand up.

A man from Illinois

We both embrace and mourn the demythologiz-
ing of so very much of our Christian tradition [in
Jesus: A Revolutionary Biography]. At one point
one of us said, "He's taken away Christmas, he's
taken away the miracles and now he's taking away
Easter as well." We cannot help wondering if the
glorious music and art these tales have inspired
would have resulted if those Biblical passages had
been seen as just "stories." However, we are also
aware that you haven't really taken them away. In

some sense it is possible to embrace their truth more
fully now that the stories are not burdened with a lit-
eralism they cannot sustain.

A group in Ohio

Most of us have not thought of Jesus as a peasant
leading—in effect—a social revolution. This vision
of Jesus covers equality, justice, non-discrimination,
healing and management power. Yes, we know this is
the work of Christianity, but how often do we think
of Jesus "leading the charge."

A woman from Illinois

With all sincerity we would like for you to consider the following questions: Were you alive when
Jesus performed his ministry? Were you present at
his crucifixion and burial? Were you present at his
resurrection? If you were not, how can you consider yourself to be an authority on what took place
and why it took place? . . . We do not consider
ourselves to be authorities, but we believe in his
physical resurrection as witnessed by many who
were there.

A group from Illinois

If Jesus as the rural, Jewish version of the philosophical Cynic School is a personal model, how can
we authentically have possessions, live in relative
comfort, hold steady institutional jobs, and get
married?

A man from Arizona

> *Through my high school and particularly my college years . . . I just could not accept so much of the mythology surrounding the gospels and the life of Jesus that I heard in church. . . . The two books of yours fulfill the need of mine to find out what the real Jesus taught and lived. I was absolutely fascinated and couldn't put them down. . . . After reading the books, I am struck by the fact that the real message of Jesus is probably the hardest one to really follow and live, that is, opening one's heart to society's outcasts, healing and eating with people who have little or nothing of material wealth. But at least now, my soul tells me I'm on the right track.*
>
> *A man from Virginia*

Did Jesus intend to found a new religion, the one we now call Christianity, or at least to create a separate Christian church?

The answer to that is an emphatic no, but that does not mean Jesus did not have a very specific program. He was more than just a visionary with an idea about God. He also intended to assist others in living the life demanded by that God. Jesus' intention was to restore a peasant community that was under acute strain from Roman colonization and urbanization. He did that by announcing a divine ideal, a God of radical justice in a kingdom of utter equality. I take your question to ask whether Jesus had a monopoly on that kingdom or whether it

entailed a social program available to all who
wanted to participate in its presence.

I have emphasized throughout this book that Jesus
came from a peasant class. It now becomes important
to take a closer look at what that means in terms of
Jesus' mission as a program.

We need to begin by recognizing that peasant
classes—particularly, as in first-century Palestine,
when under the heel of an oppressive power—must
make critical decisions about how to resist. And resist
they will—in one way or another. Anthropologists
distinguish between open or extraordinary and hidden
or ordinary forms of peasant resistance. We tend to
think only of *overt* resistance appearing in such
actions as revolt or rebellion. But these are usually
last-ditch desperate efforts and usually doomed to
disastrous failure. There is also, however, *covert* resistance, that everyday reaction which stays just below
the surface and cannot therefore be so easily detected,
readily punished, or effectively eliminated. Everything
from minor sabotage, theft, or arson, to acting dumb,
making mistakes, or misunderstanding orders consti-
tute the everyday and ordinary forms of protest which
maintain the dignity of the oppressed without inviting
lethal punishment.

That distinction helps us sort out peasant
responses to Roman rule in the first-century Jewish
homeland. There, as elsewhere, resistance did not usually begin with outright revolt—although that is often
the point where oppressors first noticed the problem.
Certainly there were *overt* forms of resistance: unarmed
protesters, armed bandits, apocalyptic prophets, and

messianic leaders. We have detailed descriptions of such forms of resistance and revolt from the aristocratic historian Josephus—because such elite observers pay attention to open and obvious forms of resistance. But *overt* resistance is always only the tip of the iceberg of peasant unrest. Most of that unrest is *covert*, hidden below the surface, and not visible to the powers against which it is aimed.

Perhaps I may use an illustration from my own background. The story presumes, centuries before, the exile of the Irish aristocracy and its replacement by British elites. A lost English huntsman in late-nineteenth-century Donegal asks an Irish peasant, "Did the gentry pass this way, my good man?" "They did that, your honor." "How long ago?" "About three hundred years ago, your honor." That is an example of a very small, relatively safe act of resistance—repeatable as story over and over again.

My argument about the mission of Jesus is this: That *what he was doing was located exactly on the borderline between overt and covert resistance.* On the one hand, his resistance was not as overt as that of protesters, prophets, bandits, or messiahs. On the other hand, it was far more overt than merely playing dumb, imagining revenge, or retelling stories from the times of Moses or David. His open eating and free healing were at the precise borderline between covert and overt, secret and open, private and public resistance. But I insist that it was nonetheless a mission of resistance.

*Was that resistance, in your opinion, a purely
personal response on Jesus' part, or was he trying
to organize a social movement? Did he try to
enlist other people in his mission?*

I can accept the term "mission" to describe what
Jesus was up to because it was more than merely a personal lifestyle. Of course, I don't mean to read into the
word "mission" the whole enterprise, for example, of
Paul's journeys throughout the Mediterranean world,
much less any theology of later Christian evangelizing.
But it is clear to me that Jesus had a magnificent
vision of the Kingdom of God here on earth and lived
that vision out. What is clear to me also is that he
empowered other persons to be actively involved with
him in that mission. You remember how John the
Baptist organized a community of the baptized spread
out across the Jewish homeland waiting for the action
of the avenging God. I think that Jesus also was orga-
nizing a movement—but with a very different message
from a very different God. Call it a companionship of
empowerment.

Can you say briefly what that mission was?

I have already described Jesus' practice of an open
table and free healing. I think his mission was basically this: to invite others into that style of life as a
challenge and empowerment. The heart of the original Jesus movement was sharing an open table and
offering free healing. That combination of shared

material resources (eating) and shared spiritual
resources (healing) is absolutely at the core of Jesus'
mission. That process involved a radically different
spirituality. It sought to bring individuals together
into a community which experienced God in that
companionship, but not just through that companionship. Instead of the hierarchy of patrons and
brokers, mediators and intermediaries which structured Mediterranean society and religion, Jesus lived
an open and direct relationship with God and invited
others to do likewise. The Kingdom of God was not a
program for isolated individuals; it was for communal
life empowering participants into direct contact with
God rather than becoming itself a substitute for that
challenge.

Take a look with me at one of the major texts
referring to this mission:

> [Jesus] said, "The harvest is abundant, but the workers
> are few; beg therefore the master of the harvest to send
> out workers into his harvest. Go. Look, I send you out as
> lambs among wolves. Do not carry money, or bag, or
> sandals, [or staff]; and do not greet anyone on the road.
>
> "Whatever house you enter, say, 'Peace be to this
> house.' And if a child of peace is there, your peace will
> rest upon him. But if not, let your peace return to you.
> And stay in the same house, eating and drinking what-
> ever they provide, for the worker deserves his wages [in
> Luke; but in Matthew: food]. Do not go from house to
> house.
>
> "And if you enter a town and they receive you, eat
> what is set before you. Heal the sick and say to

them, 'God's kingdom has come near to you.' But if
you enter a town and they do not receive you, as you
leave, shake the dust from your feet and say,
'Nevertheless, be sure of this, the realm of God has
come to you.' (Luke 10:2–11, emphasis added)

There are several questions we need to ask about
this text. The first is: Who is Jesus sending out on this
mission? The *Gospel of Thomas* simply says "followers";
the *Q Gospel* refers to "seventy others"; and Mark
refers to "the twelve apostles." My answer to our question is that those whom Jesus sent out were not from a
specific, closed group. But they were probably not so
much those who had voluntarily given up everything
as those who had recently lost everything. They were
located along that terrible divide between poverty and
destitution. It was there that the processes of Roman
urbanization pressed most heavily on the peasantry.
Not every peasant was becoming destitute, but peasant life was becoming very insecure and unstable. I
suggest, in other words, that Jesus created a *network of
shared healing* just as John had created a network of
shared apocalyptic expectation.

There is one special point I want to make in this
discussion of the "who." When Mark tells the story, he
has Jesus sending out the Twelve, *two by two*. We need
to ask why. If I may look ahead to a highly symbolic
story that we will study more closely in the chapter on
Easter—the Emmaus Road story—we may find a clue
to the meaning of missionaries in pairs. In that story
two followers of Jesus traveled from Jerusalem to
Emmaus on Easter Sunday. One of them is given a

name, Cleopas, a male. The other person is left unnamed. With any such pair in Mediterranean society, when the first person is named (male) and the second is unnamed, we may assume that the second person is a *woman*. Notice, however, that she is not identified as being Cleopas' wife. How are we to understand this pairing?

When Paul is discussing his own missionary activities (1 Corinthians 9:5), he writes: "Do we not have the right to be accompanied by a believing wife, as do the other apostles and the brothers of the Lord and Cephas?"

The literal meaning in the Greek language, "sister wife," was translated into English as "believing wife."

But Paul was, in fact, unmarried. My proposal is that "sister wife" refers not to a partner in marriage, but to a female missionary who travels with a male missionary as if, for the world at large, she is his wife. Why this pairing? The obvious answer is that it would provide social protection for a traveling female missionary in a world of male power and violence. I suggest that was the original purpose of Jesus' sending missionaries out in pairs—namely, to allow for female missionaries. That male/female partnership in mission has obvious significance, not only for understanding Jesus' intention, but also for the role of women in modern Christianity.

Part of that mission passage quoted above is here worth a careful look: "Do not carry money, or bag, or sandals [or staff]; and do not greet anyone on the road." This is a picture of what you might call "the dress code" of the Kingdom movement.

A dress code for the Kingdom of God?

Actually, yes—and a fairly strict one at that. But
the point, of course, is the symbolism of the dress
code. In fact, as you read later versions of this story
(for example, in the gospel of Mark), you'll find that
this more radical dress code is made more lenient.
Whereas here the missionaries are told not to carry
money, or bag, or sandals, or staff, Mark *allows* them to
carry a staff and sandals. Wherever we see more strin-
gent or radical requirements being watered down, we
may be confident that time has passed and the Church
is adjusting the lifestyle of the historical Jesus to its
own later needs. So I conclude that the forbidding of
purse, bag, sandals, staff, and greetings are basic and
original, coming from Jesus himself.

What was Jesus' point in making such strict rules about dress and behavior on the road?

To get some clues, let me take you around the
Mediterranean Sea for a look at other radical first-
century missionaries who, like Jesus, preached to ordinary people both by what they said and how they
lived, by what they taught and how they dressed. I
refer to the philosophical movement called Cynicism.

Nowadays we use the word "cynicism" to mean
belief in nothing or doubt about everything. What it
meant in the first century was not simply philosophical disbelief, but also a practical resistance to ordinary
cultural values. The Cynics tried to find happiness

through freedom from desires, emotions, controls, authorities, public opinion, property, family life. Their symbolic dress code involved carrying a knapsack, holding a staff, and wearing a dirty, ragged cloak which left the right shoulder bare. They usually did not wear shoes and their hair and beards were long and disheveled. You would not be far wrong to see here a picture of first-century *hippies*, dramatizing in dress their refusal to accept society's material values. Cynicism was thus a resistance movement against conventional society—and particularly involved a questioning of power, rule, dominion, and kingship. You may remember the famous story in which the Cynic Diogenes, invited by Alexander the Great to name anything he wanted, asked the conqueror simply to get out of his sunlight. That famous story raises the question: Who is the true ruler, the one who wants everything or the one who needs nothing? Who is really wealthy: the one who wants all of Asia or the one content with just a little sunlight? The Cynics, whose life and dress were a form of street theater among the ordinary people, thus profoundly questioned the assumptions of their culture and, indeed, of civilization.

But if the Cynics around the Mediterranean sound something like the Jesus movement—both agree about wearing no sandals and spending no time on ordinary greetings and gossip along the road—they also have some flat-out disagreements. And here we need especially to talk about wallet and staff.

Actually that term "wallet" is an unfortunate translation, since for us it connotes money. The Greek

word would be better translated as "knapsack." What
it symbolized for the Cynics was their complete self-
sufficiency; that is, they carried their homes and possessions with them. All they needed could be carried
in a simple knapsack slung over the shoulder. So also
with the staff. It represented their itinerant status, the
fact that they were always spiritually on the way elsewhere. So knapsack and staff symbolized their itinerant self-sufficiency.

By contrast, the Jesus missionaries are told precisely to carry *no* knapsack and hold *no* staff in their
hands. This is a striking difference, and we need to ask
what it means. I think it means this: whereas the
Cynics are emphasizing *self-sufficiency*, the Jesus missionaries are emphasizing *communal dependency*. The
Cynics need no one and nothing; the Jesus missionaries need their food and lodging from others with
whom they share the open table and free healing.
Both groups are itinerant, but whereas the Cynics are
self-sufficient loners, the missionaries sent out by Jesus
are dependent upon a new community.

Are you suggesting that Jesus adopted some of his ideas from the Cynic movement?

We really have no way of knowing whether Jesus
had even heard about the Cynic movement. The
point I'm making is not that Jesus either borrowed
from or imitated that movement, but that it's instruc-
tive to see how both Jesus and the Cynic preachers
appealed to the ordinary people. Both were lifestyle

preachers advocating their positions not only by word, but by deed; both symbolized their messages dramatically by dress; both Jesus and the Cynics taught and acted against materialism, oppression, and a distorted sense of what made for real power in the first century. The differences, of course, are also striking. The Cynic was urban, while Jesus was rural; the Cynic followed an individual philosophy of self-sufficiency, while Jesus organized a communal movement; Cynic symbolism demanded knapsack and staff, that of Jesus no knapsack and no staff. Perhaps it is not too much to say that Jesus is what peasant Jewish Cynicism might have looked like. In any case, and even if Jesus had never heard of the Cynics, the comparison helps me understand the meaning of that dress code.

Can you explain more fully that combination of free healing and open eating?

What I see is an interaction between the itinerant missionaries whom Jesus sends out and the householders who receive them into their homes. I think of Jesus' program as a peasant movement aimed precisely at the frightening line between the destitute and the poor, between those who had lost their land and those who were still managing a subsistence living on it. The background to such debt foreclosure, land loss, and impoverishment was, of course, the booming economy of the early first century's *Pax Romana*. This showed up in Lower Galilee as two new walled cities of about twenty-five thousand inhabitants each, one

rebuilt after destruction (Sepphoris) and another built
from scratch (Tiberias) within twenty years and
twenty miles of one another in the first twenty years
of Jesus' life. Imagine what those cities did to peasant
life and land in the surrounding countryside.
Itinerants and householders were often just steps
apart, on either side of that terrible line (as some of
our American homed and homeless are today).

Jesus' program attempted to rebuild peasant life
from its grass roots upwards by bringing those two
classes, the destitute and the poor, more even than the
poor and the rich, into interaction with each other.
The Kingdom of God appears in that interaction
because it resides, not just with the itinerants, but
with the relationship between itinerants and householders. One group, the itinerants, must move beyond
envy and hate; the other group, the householders,
must move beyond fear and terror. One needs eating,
the other healing; and at a certain point, eating and
healing become one.

*What about us? To be a real Christian, are we
also supposed to adopt a counter-culture, itinerant lifestyle? That doesn't seem very practical.*

Good question. Think back to that distinction
between *itinerants* and *householders*. When the itinerant missionaries come into a village and accept hospi-
tality from the more settled householders, the
householders are not told just to drop everything and
hit the road. After all, the message of the itinerants is,

"The Kingdom of God has come to you." The house-holders, too, experience the Kingdom as shared eating and healing *right where they are*.

Very early on, we can sense some tension between the itinerants and the householders. A first-century document called the *Didache* (the word means "teaching") expresses the viewpoint of the householders. They're told, for example: "Do not judge the prophets (i.e. the itinerants), but do not imitate them either." It's okay to live out the Kingdom vision in your village. And they're also told, "if you can bear the whole yoke of the Lord, you will be perfect, but if you cannot, do what you can."

"Do what you can." I think that is an important part of the answer to your question. To be a Christian is to live in the tension between Jesus' radical message/lifestyle and the requirements of daily life for most of us. Meeting Jesus is a little bit like watching Michael Jordan play basketball. You're probably not going to be a Michael Jordan, but you see in him amazing possibilities for the human body—and maybe you start treating your own more respectfully. In a similar way, in Jesus we see new possibilities for human living. When we take him seriously, we live in a creative tension between the requirements of our usual life (like settled householders) and the radical challenge of living counter-culturally (like the itinerants on the road). I think also of a Washington, D.C., activist working on the overwhelming problem of world hunger. Someone asked him how he keeps at it without throwing in the towel and giving up. "You have to have two things," he answered. "One is a

vision. The second is an ability to celebrate small vic-
tories." That's not a bad way to express the tension
between the ideal and present reality. Like those for
whom the *Didache* was written, we who have to go to
work from eight o'clock to five o'clock, change dirty
diapers, and pay the orthodontist, need to hear this
message: "Do what you can."

Before we leave the subject of Jesus' missionary
movement, I want to call your attention once again to
the passage in which the missionaries are sent out. You
may have noticed that Luke says, ". . . and stay in the
same house, eating and drinking whatever they provide *for the worker deserves his wages*"; in Matthew's
version it is "the worker deserves his *food*." I think
that something important is at stake in this difference
between *food* and *wages*.

What we have here is a transition from food in the
context of the open table to food as payment. It seems
to be a development that occurred as the Jesus movement became more institutionalized—and perhaps the
shift was necessary. But if the mission was becoming
more efficient, better organized, and more adapted to
urban rather than rural realities, it was also becoming
a different mission in the process. What I argue is that
the open table was not for Jesus merely a strategy for
supporting the mission, a way of "paying" those sent
out. The open table was, rather, a strategy for building
peasant community at the grassroots level. For that
reason any move from *food shared* to *wages due* was a
momentous step in the movement's development. It
was a step from new community to institution, from
movement to church.

7

Who Executed Jesus and Why?

I write to express to you my grateful thanks for your excellent and most readable research and books into the historical Jesus. I have found them to be exciting, challenging and revealing. I have "grown" as a minister of the Church of Scotland through these works.

A man from Scotland

I hope others tell you that your effort to be both scholarly and honest is greatly admirable. I very much appreciate your writing and courage. I hope the critical voices do not inhibit you. I could not put down Jesus: A Revolutionary Biography until I finished it. Too few are able to sit with and work through the moral clash (between the historian and the believer). But for those who can, please press on. As an Episcopal priest I have long felt alone in an unthinking world. I do not feel so alone now. Thank you very much.

A man from Illinois

I love to go to the Carmelite Convent to pray but what would they think if they knew that I don't believe Jesus is the only Son of God (if he is, then who am I? Adopted from the Martians, maybe?) And I don't believe that God asked anyone to suffer a cruel, cruel, violent death for me or anyone so that he could be expiated.

A woman from Illinois

I want you to know that your book The Historical Jesus: The Life of a Mediterranean Jewish Peasant *. . . set me on a quest. . . . As one well on the road to the Episcopal priesthood I have spent countless sleepless hours attempting to reach some rational resolve to how best to balance the highly Eucharistic and liturgical creeds and other expressions of our faith in light of all that "higher criticism" and Christology would cast into doubt. Today I finished your* Four Other Gospels. *Where do I find the continuity and the way to understand the juncture between faith and reason, historicity and ecclesiology?*

A man from Georgia

God sent Him as a sacrifice for all sin—once and for all—so that sinful man need not go once a year to give animals' blood for their sins—Also because of his coming into the world, anyone and everyone could be saved from the death that Adam and Eve caused to be brought upon mankind.

A woman from North Carolina

A few months ago I was asked to address a study class in a local Lutheran church. . . . I asked the group, "Why was Jesus killed?" After a long pause, one of the few men in attendance said, "So that we can be saved." I replied, "No, that wasn't the reason. He was killed because he was a troublemaker, a rabble-rouser. He was threatening the authority and the income of the existing clergy and government leaders."

A woman from Pennsylvania

You said Jesus taught radical egalitarianism and demanded itinerancy. As to social and political equality no he didn't. In the 17th chapter of John, Jesus plainly stated his kingdom was no part of this world. He refused kingship. That is one reason why the Romans hated the Jews. The Jews claimed that Jesus would rule this earth from Jerusalem. That claim proved false just as it does today. The kingdom is heavenly and it is ruling now!! Soon now your religion and all others except one will be destroyed.

A man from Canada

I think that the members of the Jesus Seminar should realize the seriousness of "peeling away" the New Testament. The Bible is planned out in such a wonderful way that everything fits together perfectly, New Testament and Old Testament alike. God has a special purpose for every single verse in the Bible so I think every verse should remain just how it is. I did not write this letter to scold or offend anyone. I did write it to tell you that Jesus Christ died on the cross

to bring people close to God again. Immanuel means
"God with us." No matter what any historical facts
or experts say, I know this is true because He is with
me right now as my savior and closest friend.

                              A woman from Michigan

What was crucifixion and why did people get crucified in the ancient world?

That Jesus "was crucified under Pontius Pilate," as
the creed states, is as certain as anything historical can
ever be. The Jewish historian Josephus and the pagan
historian Tacitus both agree that Jesus was executed
by order of the Roman governor of Judea. And it is
very hard to imagine that Jesus' first followers would
have invented such a story unless it had indeed happened. While the brute *fact* of Jesus' death by crucifixion is historically certain, however, those detailed
narratives in our present gospels are much more problematic. They are far, far less historically certain. One
other preliminary point. To look without flinching at
crucifixion is painful, not only for those who have
faith in Jesus, but also for those who simply have faith
in humanity. Crucifixion was a cruel instrument of
state terror.

Let me begin by describing crucifixion as practiced
in the ancient world. One contemporary scholar has
summarized the evidence as follows (Martin Hengel,
Crucifixion, 86–88). I cite it here to invite your reading of the entire book as a detailed catalog of horror.

Crucifixion as a penalty was remarkably widespread in antiquity. It appears in various forms among numerous peoples of the ancient world, even among the Greeks. . . . [It] was and remained a political and military punishment. While among the Persians and the Carthaginians it was imposed primarily on high officials and commanders, as on rebels, among the Romans it was inflicted above all on the lower classes, i.e., slaves, violent criminals, and the unruly elements in rebellious provinces, not least in Judea. The chief reason for its use was its allegedly supreme efficacy as a deterrent; it was, of course, carried out publicly. . . . It was usually associated with other forms of torture, including at least flogging. . . . By the public display of a naked victim at a prominent place—at a crossroads, in the theater, on high ground, at the place of his crime—crucifixion also represented his uttermost humiliation. . . . Crucifixion was aggravated further by the fact that quite often its victims were never buried. It was a stereotyped picture that the crucified victim served as food for wild beasts and birds of prey. In this way his humiliation was made complete. What it meant for a man in antiquity to be refused burial, and the dishonour which went with it, can hardly be appreciated by modern man.

Notice those words about the lack of burial in cases of crucifixion. Not to allow burial attempted utterly to annihilate the human being.

*I heard some time ago about the discovery of a
first-century crucified skeleton. Is that correct?*

In June of 1968 the only skeleton of a crucified
person ever uncovered in the Jewish homeland was
found in Jerusalem in a tomb that dates from the
first century. It was found among the bones of
thirty-five individuals whose deaths, by the way,
offer a glimpse of the harshness of first-century life.
Ten of those thirty-five individuals had died tragi-
cally. A woman and her infant had died together in
childbirth; three children had died of starvation;
five people had met violent deaths—two by burning, one by a blow from a mace-like weapon, a child
by an arrow wound, and a male in his twenties by
crucifixion. The name of the crucified man was
Yehochanan. His arms had not been nailed, but
tied, to the bar of the cross, probably with his arms
to the elbows hung over and behind it. His legs had
been placed on either side of the upright beam,
with nails holding his heel bones to the wood on
either side. There was no evidence that the man's
legs had been broken, which was sometimes done
in crucifixions, causing a speedier death by asphyx-
iation because the chest would cave in.

Crucifixion, as we have seen, was widely used in
the ancient world and, by the Romans especially,
inflicted on unruly elements in rebellious provinces
like Judea. We know, for example, that the Syrian
governor, Varus, needed three legions as well as auxil-
iary troops to put down revolts in the Jewish homeland, including three major messianic uprisings after

the death of Herod the Great and around the time of Jesus' birth. According to Josephus, when Varus arrived in Jerusalem, he crucified two thousand rebels. Josephus also tells us that in the year 66, at the start of the first Roman-Jewish War, the Roman governor Florus had about thirty-six hundred Jewish children, women, and men scourged and crucified in a single day. Four years later, when Titus's army circled Jerusalem, many who had fled the city in search of food were caught, tortured, and crucified—according to Josephus, five hundred or more every day. My reason for listing examples of the widespread horror of crucifixion is to raise the obvious question: Why, with so many thousands crucified in the first century around Jerusalem, has only a single skeleton been found?

The reason is clear, and it is terrible to contemplate. The three supreme Roman penalties were crucifixion, burning, and death by wild beasts. What made them supreme was not just their inhuman cruelty or their public dishonor, but the fact that there might be nothing left of a person to bury at the end. The bodily destruction in being cast into the fire or thrown to the beasts is obvious enough, but what we often don't realize about crucifixion is the carrion crow who croaks above the cross and the scavenger dogs who growl beneath the dead or dying bodies. Greco-Roman authors who wrote on the subject mentioned the crucified ones as "evil food for birds of prey and grim pickings for dogs." That was the harsh reality of crucifixion in the first century.

*But what on earth did Jesus do to end up cruci-
fied—particularly if that fate was reserved for
rebels—since he avoided open resistance to
Roman rule?*

That's a difficult question, and it will take some
time for us to sort out.

We begin with the tradition of the gospels that say
Jesus was crucified around the time of Passover.
Although the gospel writers disagree on the precise
timing, I see no reason not to accept as historical the
general connection of Jesus' death with the Passover
festival.

Remember what Passover was about. It was a celebration of the deliverance of the Jews from slavery in
Egypt and their liberation as they moved toward the
Promised Land. Obviously, that was a festival with
very dangerous overtones in a colonized country under
foreign yoke. It wouldn't have taken much imagination for first-century Jews to identify contemporary
Romans with the ancient Egyptians from whose domination they had been set free. We know that huge
crowds came together in a very concentrated space in
Jerusalem. When Josephus wrote about an earlier
Passover celebration after the death of Herod the
Great, he mentioned "an innumerable multitude of
people [who] come down from the country and even
from abroad to worship God." That particular phrase
appears in the context of an episode in which the
assembled crowds resisted the troops of Archelaus, one
of Herod's heirs, who thereupon attacked them with
the result that about three thousand worshipers were

slaughtered in the Temple precincts. That incident demonstrates how explosive a situation Passover could be: Crowds gathered amid present oppression to celebrate deliverance from ancient oppression. At Passover time Pilate brought extra troops from Caesarea to the Antonia fortress overlooking the Temple courts. He was fully prepared to stop any trouble before it could even begin, and this explosive situation is the historical context of Jesus' arrest and death.

But that still doesn't answer the question of what Jesus did to get himself arrested and crucified.

Let us look at two separate incidents from the days immediately before Jesus' arrest, to see which might best explain what happened to him.

First, there is the story of what we usually call the "triumphal entry into Jerusalem" on what is now celebrated as Palm Sunday.

> *And they brought the colt to Jesus, and threw their garments on it; and he sat upon it. And many spread their garments on the road, and others spread leafy branches which they had cut from the fields. And those who went before and those who followed cried out, "Hosanna! Blessed is he who comes in the name of the Lord! Blessed is the kingdom of our father David that is coming! Hosanna in the highest."* (Mark 11:7–10)

Implicitly in Mark, and explicitly in Matthew and John, that action of Jesus is seen to be a fulfillment of a prophecy in Zachariah 9:9:

> *Lo, your king comes to you;*
> *triumphant and victorious is he,*
> *humble and riding on an ass,*
> *on a colt the foal of an ass.*

Certainly such a symbolic action born of messianic hopes could have provoked a repressive response from the authorities who, I have mentioned, were on heightened alert at Passover time. But the fact that it so specifically fulfills a prophetic passage makes me suspicious of its historical validity. As we have often seen, later Christian scribes looked backward to cull from the Hebrew scriptures passages that might interpret the ministry of Jesus—and sometimes those passages become the inspiration for actually creating events. So I personally doubt that the entry into Jerusalem ever actually happened.

A much more likely reason for Jesus' arrest is found in the story of the *Temple disturbance*. Here we are on much more solid historical ground; indeed, we have three independent sources for this incident.

Here is Mark's version (11:15–19) of the Temple disturbance:

> *And they came to Jerusalem. And he entered the temple and began to drive out those who sold and those who bought in the temple, and he overturned the tables of the money-changers and the seats of those*

> who sold pigeons; and he would not allow any one to
> carry anything through the temple.
>
> And he taught, and said to them, "Is it not written,
> 'My house shall be called a house of prayer for all the
> nations' [=Isaiah 56:7]? But you have made it a den
> of robbers [=Jeremiah 7:11]."

As I look at this story in comparison with other versions (for example in John, and the *Gospel of Thomas*), I conclude that Mark described the action of Jesus in the Temple but added to it his own scripture references (from Isaiah and Jeremiah) by way of interpretation. A version in the *Gospel of Thomas* contains a saying that more likely came from the historical Jesus. Jesus said, "I shall [destroy this] house and no one will be able to build it." That is, *Jesus was symbolically destroying the Temple.*

This trip was probably the only one Jesus ever took to Jerusalem. His vision of open table and free healing clashed wildly with what he saw in the Temple, the seat and symbol of everything that was patronal, hierarchical, brokered, even oppressive on both the religious and political level. The Temple was in the hands of high priests who were not of legitimate lineage according to Jewish law, but were hired and fired like servants by the Romans and Herodians, whose puppets they had become. Jesus' symbolic act of destruction reinforced what he had been teaching, what he had expressed through his healings, what he had effected in his practice of open eating and drinking. It was like going into a draft office during the Vietnam War and pouring blood over drawers of file cards, or

like climbing a fence at a missile site and hammering
on the nosecone of an ICBM. It was a symbolic nega-
tion of everything the institution stood for. No doubt
Jesus' activities in Galilee might have led to his arrest
at any time. But especially in the tinderbox atmosphere of the Temple at Passover time, with Pilate's
forces keeping close watch, Jesus' challenge was suffi-
cient to cause the soldiers to move in to arrest him.

Let me emphasize two points. Jesus was not
"cleansing" the Temple; nor was his action some
Christianity *versus* Judaism scenario. The Temple
was and had to be the seat of collaboration with
the Roman occupation authority. The High Priest
had to be, whether he liked it or not, the link
between his colonized people and their imperial
overlords. In such a situation, any Jew—even, or
especially, an absolutely fervent Essene or an absolutely observant Pharisee—could have performed
an action like that of Jesus. It was a symbolic
destruction of the Temple as hopelessly and irrevo-
cably contaminated and compromised. Was it the
house of prayer and sacrifice or the seat of collaboration and oppression? Was the High Priest legitimate or even valid and what did such invalidity do
to the house of God?

*You refer to the phrase in the creed about Jesus
being "crucified under Pontius Pilate," and you
mention his soldiers moving in to arrest Jesus.
But didn't Pilate actually try to wash his hands
of the whole affair?*

In the New Testament accounts, as you suggested, Pilate is portrayed as being completely just and fair, desiring to acquit Jesus but forced reluctantly and against his will to crucify him because of the insistence of Jewish authorities and the Jerusalem crowd. But what we have learned about Pontius Pilate from other records is totally at variance with that benign picture. We know quite a bit about the historical Pilate. We have archaeological as well as literary evidence for Pilate. In 1961 in the amphitheater at Caesarea a dedicatory stone to the Emperor Tiberius was found bearing the inscription "Pontius Pilate, prefect of Judea." He governed for ten years in Judea, from the years 26 to 36—a lengthy period for a second-level Roman administrator. And Josephus has told us a number of stories about Pilate's rule.

He tells us, for example, that when Pilate brought his army from Caesarea to Jerusalem for winter quarters, under cover of darkness he introduced into the city embossed medallions of the emperor attached to the military standards. This incensed the Jews, for whom the making of images was forbidden. Outraged ordinary citizens of Jerusalem walked to Caesarea and begged Pilate to remove the offending emblems. When he refused, they engaged in a sit-down strike for five days and nights around his palace. Pilate summoned the demonstrators to a stadium for an audience where he surrounded them with soldiers and threatened to kill them all unless they went home. But when the whole crowd offered their necks to the sword rather than compromise their faith, it was Pilate himself who was forced to yield rather than risk

a massacre that might get unwelcome attention in
Rome.

On another occasion Pilate provoked an uproar by
confiscating money from the sacred treasure of the
Temple in order to construct an aqueduct. This time
he was smarter; he infiltrated an angry crowd with disguised soldiers in civilian dress with orders not to use
their swords, but to beat the rioters with cudgels. So
much for Pilate's gentle methods of crowd control.

In another incident Pilate had to deal not with
massed protesters, but apocalyptic prophets. A group
of Samaritans gathered at the sacred Mount Gerizim,
apparently expecting an apocalyptic demonstration of
God's power. Pilate suppressed the movement with a
heavy hand, killing some, scattering others, and
putting to death a number of leaders and prisoners. In
fact, his methods were so harsh that the Syrian legate
Vitellius sent Pilate off to Rome to explain himself.
Even by Roman standards, therefore, Pilate was judged
to be excessively cruel and unnecessarily brutal. So it
is impossible for me to take as historically accurate a
New Testament portrayal of Pilate as a reluctant,
innocent bystander in a tragedy not of his making.

But didn't he offer to release Jesus—but the people asked for Barabbas instead?

I regard that narrative as absolutely unhistorical.
First, the picture of Pilate meekly acquiescing to a
shouting crowd is exactly the opposite of what we
know about him from both the Jewish historian

Josephus, just mentioned, and also from the contemporary Jewish philosopher, Philo of Alexandria, who used him as the model of a bad governor. Brutal crowd control was his specialty. Second, we have no evidence of a custom of open amnesty, namely, the releasing of any requested prisoner at the time of the Passover festival. The Barabbas incident did not actually happen. But I think we can readily understand why Mark created such a story.

We have talked about various kinds of resisters in the Jewish homeland: protesters, apocalyptic prophets, messianic claimants. There was one other group of peasant resisters in the first-century Jewish homeland—*rebel bandits*. Who were they? They were peasants forced off their farms who took to the hills and banditry rather than to the roads and beggary. They were not ordinary, but *social bandits*—whom other peasants might well have regarded as freedom fighters. Where you find rebel bandits you can be sure that the oppressed lower classes are being pushed below even subsistence level and forced into armed resistance, however ineffective or desperate.

There is a precise word in Greek for such a rebel bandit and that is exactly what Barabbas is called in Mark's story. He is a rebel, an insurgent, a freedom fighter. Mark wrote soon after the end of the first Roman-Jewish War when Jerusalem and its Temple had been totally destroyed in the year 70. In this story, he expressed symbolically his interpretation of that catastrophe. Among those who had carried on the futile struggle against Rome were Zealots, a loose coalition of bandit groups and peasant rebels. What

Mark is saying in this story is: such was Jerusalem's choice, Barabbas over Jesus, an armed rebel over an unarmed savior. The Barabbas story was a symbolic dramatization of Jerusalem's fate *as Mark saw it*. It tells us nothing about Jesus' trial, but it tells us much about Mark's theological perspective on the (much later) fall of Jerusalem.

But don't we have a very careful historical record of Jesus' last week? After all, we have almost an hour-by-hour account there of his trials and the events of the crucifixion.

As I mentioned at the start of this chapter, part of the difficulty in dealing with the events around the crucifixion is that the *fact* of the crucifixion is historically certain, but the *narratives* are very problematic. And the reason is clear. Remember how searching the scriptures created the infancy narratives that we found in Matthew and Luke? In a similar way Christian imagination took the fact of Jesus' crucifixion and fleshed it out by searching the scriptures to provide not only a rationale for his fate, but specific narratives telling its story.

Are you saying that we can't trust the gospel writers—that they are just making up stories as they go along?

I'm not suggesting that they're writing fiction in a modern sense. They were engaged in a style of religious reflection that was common to Judaism in the first century. For instance, we have all heard of the Dead Sea Scrolls. Those Scrolls, discovered in 1947, tell us about the community life of a first-century Jewish sect whose home at Qumran was destroyed during the first Roman-Jewish War. They began as a priest-led group who withdrew from Jerusalem's Temple and fled to the wilderness, believing that the Temple had been polluted by false leadership. From their long-lost library we have learned a great deal about their community and—this is my point in referring to them now about their way of interpreting scripture.

As the Qumran scribes applied the Hebrew Bible to their present situation, they interwove the ancient texts with their contemporary interpretations so densely that it is hard for us to tell when Bible leaves off and commentary begins. Trying to follow their interpretive work is enough to make your head spin. I won't go into too much detail, but I do want you to understand that the texts and the history could begin to interweave and to mutually influence one another. I am suggesting that a similar process occurred among some of Jesus' followers.

Two examples. The story of soldiers casting lots for Jesus' garments (see Mark 15:24) was developed from a Psalm that was often used by Christians to interpret Jesus' death:

They divide my clothes among themselves,
and for my clothing they cast lots. (Psalm 22:18)

And the story (variously told) of the suffering Jesus being given gall or poison for food, and vinegar or soured wine for drink (see Matthew 27:34) comes from another Psalm:

They gave me poison for food,
and for my thirst they gave me vinegar to drink.
(Psalm 69:21)

In the same way, other details of the crucifixion story—for instance, the spitting on and mocking of Jesus, the crown of thorns, the two thieves crucified with him, darkness at noon—all were created out of Old Testament texts.

Traditionally, Christians have said, "See how Christ's passion was foretold by the prophets." Actually, it was the other way around. The Hebrew prophets did not predict the events of Jesus' last week; rather, many of those Christian stories were created to fit the ancient prophecies in order to show that Jesus, despite his execution, was still and always held in the hands of God.

My proposal is this: Jesus' first followers knew almost nothing whatsoever about the details of his crucifixion, death, or burial. We have those detailed accounts of his final days and hours because *Old Testament texts were turned into first-century events.* That is, the Hebrew scriptures were not *predictions* of what would happen to Jesus, but were used later to *create* the stories about what happened to him; they were sought out *backwards*, as it were, after that death had occurred. Prophecy, in other words, is known after the fact rather than before it.

Recently I read an article about you in the **Detroit Free Press.** *The headline ran: "A Controversial Scholar Says Key Biblical Scenes Are Fiction that Led to Persecution of Jews." Comment?*

Nowhere is background more necessary than here. The gospels do not claim to be exact *histories* or straightforward *biographies* but *gospels*, that is, good news. Gospels must be two things: good and news. The word "good" underlines that it is from somebody's point of view, that of, say, the Christian followers of Jesus rather than the Roman authorities. The word "news" underlines the hallmark of a gospel: updating. Each gospel must not only tell the story of Jesus, it must update it for its own time and place, situation and audience. Maybe we do not like that and would prefer journalism. But whether we like it or not, gospels update. That is, of course, why we can have one Jesus but several gospels. Gospels update the words and deeds of Jesus by adopting and adapting, inventing sayings and events, debates and dialogues. So far, so good. But they also update stories of the *enemies* of Jesus, and that is where the trouble starts.

It is not as if the early Christians sat down and said, "Let us invent lies about our enemies." Christians were originally one Jewish group among many other Jewish groups in the first century. We should hear the word "Christians" the way we hear words like "Pharisees," "Sadducees," "Essenes," "Zealots," or any other group within Judaism at that time. They may all have been struggling for power and control, for the hearts and minds, the destiny and leadership of their own people. But it was all within, not against, Judaism itself. No matter what names were called or accusations made, one could hardly talk of anti-Judaism or anti-Semitism at that stage.

But, especially after the disaster of the first Roman-Jewish War, Christians were becoming more and more marginalized as a force within Judaism and were becoming less and less likely to attain the leadership of their own people. The future would lie with Rabbinic Judaism and not with Christian Judaism.

As described by Mark in the 70s, Jesus' enemies at the crucifixion are "the crowd" from Jerusalem. By Matthew in the 80s, that crowd has grown to "all the people." And by John in the 90s, it has become, quite simply, "the Jews." I do not think that even John means the Jews as distinct from non-Jews. He means: all those other bad Jews except us good Jews! It is as if some Americans were to say, "Americans are too violent," not thereby denying that they were themselves American but meaning: all those bad Americans except us good Americans.

None of that process, even in its nastiest name-calling, made much difference in the second or third centuries when Christianity, though by then a religion distinct from Judaism, had no power of reprisal. But in the fourth century, when the Roman Empire became officially Christian, those very same crucifixion stories took on the meaning of Christians accusing Jews, and began the long and lethal process that prepared Europe for the Holocaust in the terrible fullness of time.

My point in *Who Killed Jesus?* was that we must understand those crucifixion accounts and calculate especially the updating process intrinsic to gospel. We must also, as contemporary Christians, discuss responsibly what to do with the public reading and private study of those texts, lest the anti-Semitic hate they have fueled in the past continue to haunt the future. That was why the book's subtitle read: *Exposing the Roots of Anti-Semitism in the Gospel Story of the Death of Jesus.*

We've talked about what didn't happen. What do you think actually happened during those last days of Jesus' life?

My best historical reconstruction would be something like this. Jesus was arrested during the Passover festival, most likely in response to his action in the Temple. Those who were closest to him ran away for their own safety. I do not presume that there were any high-level confrontations between Caiaphas and Pilate and Herod Antipas either about Jesus or with Jesus. No doubt they would have agreed before the festival that fast action was to be taken against any disturbance and that a few examples by crucifixion might be especially useful at the outset. And I doubt very much if Jewish police or Roman soldiers needed to go too far up the chain of command in handling a Galilean peasant like Jesus. It is hard for us to imagine the casual brutality with which Jesus was probably taken and executed. All those "last week" details in our gospels, as distinct from the brute facts just mentioned, are prophecy turned into history, rather than history remembered.

You mentioned earlier that it was customary for crucified bodies to be left for the beasts. But in Jesus' case, wasn't he buried in a tomb owned by Joseph of Arimathea?

First of all, it was *possible* for a crucified body to be given back to its family for burial. That certainly was the case with the Yehochanan whom I mentioned at the beginning of this chapter. But it was very unusual. In a patronal society, getting permission for such a burial would have taken some influence. In general, if you had influence, you did not end up crucified, and if you ended up crucified, you would not have enough influence to be buried. Normally soldiers guarded the body until death, and thereafter it was left for carrion crow, scavenger dog, or other wild beast to finish the brutal job. And as I said earlier, the horror of nonburial was part of the crucifixion routine, intended by the authorities to serve as a dreadful warning to every passerby.

Of course, we cannot know with certainty what happened to the body of Jesus, but we can see clearly how much concern there was in the developing Christian tradition about the disposition of his body. The accounts steadily become more dignified and elaborate, as the horror of the brutal truth was, through hope and imagination, turned into appropriate and even regal burial.

To begin with, in the *Gospel of Peter*, a text not found in the New Testament, we are simply told that the dead Jesus was buried by those who had crucified him. That story grows out of the Jewish terror of non-burial, expressed in Deuteronomy 21:22–23:

> *When someone is convicted of a crime punishable by death and is executed, and you hang him on a tree, his corpse must not remain all night upon the tree; you shall bury him that same day, for anyone hung on a tree is under God's curse.*

Christians *hoped* that those who crucified Jesus might have buried him in deference to that ancient text. But as the tradition grew, Jesus' burial was moved from enemies to friends, from inadequate and hurried to full and complete.

That brings us to the well-known story in Mark 15:42–46:

> *When evening had come, and since it was the day of Preparation, that is, the day before the sabbath, Joseph of Arimathea, a respected member of the council, who was also himself waiting expectantly for the kingdom of God, went boldly to Pilate and asked for the body of Jesus. Then Pilate wondered if he were already dead; and summoning the centurion, he asked him whether he had been dead for some time. When he learned from the centurion that he was dead, he granted the body to Joseph. Then Joseph bought a linen cloth, and taking down the body, wrapped it in the linen cloth, and laid it in a tomb*

that had been hewn out of the rock. He then rolled a
stone against the door of the tomb.

I regard this story as the creation of Mark. (By the way, the naming of Joseph of Arimathea, as in the case of Barabbas, does not necessarily guarantee historical accuracy. If you are inventing a person, it is easy to invent a name for him as well.) Notice what Mark has done. Joseph is both "a respected member of the council"—that is, on the side of those who crucified Jesus—and also "waiting expectantly for the kingdom of God"—that is, on the side of Jesus and his followers. Matthew and Luke each try to improve on the story. Matthew describes Joseph as "a disciple of Jesus"—rather than as a member of the council that condemned Jesus. Luke keeps Joseph on the council but says that "though a member of the council, he had not agreed to their plan and action." Both Matthew and Luke are trying to solve the problem in Mark's story; namely, how is it that Joseph was both part of the council that condemned Jesus and the one who sought his body for respectful burial? Finally, when John tells the story, he combines Joseph of Arimathea with the Nicodemus who had shown up earlier in his gospel, and has them giving Jesus what we may only term a royal burial in a brand new tomb located in the midst of a garden. And now Joseph is described as a disciple of Jesus, "though a secret one because of his fear of the Jews."

As I watch the development of the burial story, I find it impossible to avoid the conclusion that we have here an intense and understandable effort to avoid the stark horror of crucifixion's final act. The worst possible horror was no burial at all, Jesus left on the cross for the scavengers. The next-best hope was burial by his enemies. But it was better not to imagine how soldiers might have done that: with lime? in a shallow grave? under a pile of stones? The next-best possibility was some authority figure deciding to bury Jesus. But that would create credibility problems and besides, unless Jesus was in a separate grave all to himself, you could not have a story about finding an empty tomb! Best of all would be to have Jesus buried by those who loved him.

But is it possible *that he was buried?*

Yes, it is possible. What I must deal with, as a historian, is *probability*. If I were giving testimony in a courtroom, and I were asked in cross-examination, "Now, Professor Crossan, isn't it *possible* that . . ." I would have to answer, "Yes—of course." In historical reconstruction we do not deal in certainties. What I have offered here—and elsewhere—is my best judgment, based on my historical research—of the most likely scenario.

As you've retold the story of Jesus' arrest and execution, it sounds very human—he challenges the powers that be in the name of a new social vision, and they crush him. But how do you get from that

to a theology claiming Jesus died to save us from our sins?

I think it helps to distinguish between three ways of looking at it—*history*, *faith*, and *theology*. The *history* is clear: Jesus died by crucifixion under the Roman governor, Pontius Pilate. People who had *faith* in Jesus found meaning in that execution—he died for *us*. A developing *theology* worked out the idea that his death made atonement for human sin. Let's take a look at each of these ideas.

The crucifixion of Jesus was a terrible shock to the hopes of those who had followed him. A shameful death was not the fate they expected for someone with whom, in open table and shared healing, they had experienced the dawning of the Kingdom of God. So they had to try to make sense of it.

Faith found meaning in the *history*. We can certainly imagine a Hindu "untouchable" in India in our own century saying of the assassinated Gandhi, "He died for me." A black garbage collector in Memphis might have said of Martin Luther King, Jr., "He died for me." Both would be speaking in a historically realistic way, for in seeking the well-being of these oppressed, marginalized groups, Gandhi and King made their own deaths almost inevitable. It is not hard to imagine a Galilean peasant, aware that Jesus' vision brought him into conflict with powerful forces, saying, "He died for me."

And they would naturally express that faith in language of their own religious tradition. Soon after Jesus' death, as we have noted before, his more learned followers began to search their scriptures for clues to its meaning. In Leviticus 16 they found a ritual for atonement, in which the High Priest would confess the people's sins over a goat, which would be sent out into the wilderness, symbolically carrying those sins away. To some Christians, that came to be a prophecy about Jesus, who bore the people's sins. Of course, that is a meaningful image only to people in a religious tradition that emphasizes *blood sacrifice*.

In other Christian communities—like the one from which we get the Q *Gospel*—such sacrificial theology had no influence. The Q community regarded Jesus as the Wisdom of God. They would have talked of his death like this: Wisdom, which comes from God, is always persecuted and destroyed—but will return. *Their* theology would be: the world's powers destroyed Jesus, but he has returned to God, and he is with us *despite his death*, as God's Wisdom. They could speak of the meaning of Jesus' death without any sacrificial metaphors at all.

What about *our* way of speaking? My problem is this: language of blood sacrifice was appropriate to people used to the sacrifices that were part of ancient temple worship, but is totally alien to our world. In our society, if anyone tried blood sacrifice of even cows or sheep or goats, we would quickly make it illegal. Moreover, an atonement theology that says God sacrificed his own son in place of humans who needed to be punished for their sins might make some Christians love Jesus, but is an obscene picture of God. It is almost heavenly child abuse, and may infect our imagination at more earthly levels as well. I do not want to express my faith through a theology that pictures God demanding blood sacrifices in order to be reconciled to us.

But the last supper and the Christian Eucharist celebrate the death of Jesus. How does that fit with all you have said?

During his life Jesus enacted the Kingdom's presence by celebrating an open table—but it was a real meal for real people and most often for those who otherwise would not have eaten at all. We might sneer and call that a pot-luck Kingdom, since we eat regularly and share, when we share, our plenty with each other. For many of the first Christians, that open table meant all the food they were sure of having. And God, they believed, was their host. But Jesus died for that vision and because of that program. Inevitably and rightly, then, that open table came both to celebrate his life and commemorate his death.

You have not mentioned anything about Peter's denial. Is that event symbolic or historical?

That story derives from Mark and is copied from him into Matthew, Luke, and John. It is told with a stylistic device characteristic of Mark, in which a second incident is sandwiched between the start and finish of a first one and the two are intended to vibrate together interpretatively. For example, Jesus curses the fig tree, Jesus "destroys" the Temple, Jesus finds the fig tree withered in Mark 11:12–20. Cursed fig tree and destroyed Temple interpret one another—for Mark. So also here, Jesus' courageous confession under trial is sandwiched between the start and finish of Peter's cowardly denials. But, of course, Peter is forgiven at the end. That sandwich is a Markan creation directed to his own community, during or after the Jewish War against Rome of 66–74. Mark's community knew all about persecution from both the Roman and the Jewish side, and this is his own consoling story: Be brave like Jesus, but even if you betray like Peter, you may still expect forgiveness. I presume that Peter ran away as did most of Jesus' companions (losing their nerve but not their faith) and this story uses him, because of his leadership status, as a model for denial forgiven. The story of Peter's denial is symbolical rather than historical.

Does the same apply to Judas' betrayal? Is that historical or not?

That is a much more difficult and delicate problem. It has been suggested that Judas-as-traitor was deliberately created as an anti-Semitic slur, since the name "Judas" means "the Jew." Such a reading could easily have arisen among pagan Christians but hardly among Jewish Christians. Jesus, for example, has a brother named Judas or Jude. Fellow Jews would hardly hear "Judas" as "the Jew" in distinction from those who were not Jews. So unless the Judas story was created rather late and in a pagan Christian environment, I cannot accept that argument. Furthermore, unlike the case of Peter's denials, (derived exclusively from Mark), Judas's betrayal is found in several other independent sources, for example, Matthew 27:3–10 and Acts 1:18–20. The role of this betrayer was probably not just to locate Jesus at night, when he could be arrested quietly, since the authorities were quite ready for a public execution. The betrayal may have involved identification and not just location. Suppose, as a pure guess, that the authorities had grabbed one of Jesus' companions after the Temple incident and needed to know who had caused the trouble. That is the sort of role I imagine for Judas. Jesus was crucified in Judea and it is not anti-Semitic to say that. Jesus was betrayed by Judas and neither is it anti-Semitic to say that. I do not think, by the way, that Judas was ever one of the Twelve Apostles. The Twelve were created only after the death of Jesus, when Peter led the mission for Jewish converts and the Twelve Apostles represented that new Israel, just as the twelve patriarchs had represented the older Israel.

8

What Happened on Easter Sunday?

Your book cleans up "the story" for me; an accomplishment basic in any effort to restore the presentation of the Christian faith to a level of credibility vital to its survival as a major moral force in the world. . . . And, in our enlightenment, bonfires need not, must not, be put to the contrived stories of Jesus' descent from David, or the Virgin Birth, the Resurrection. . . . Let us keep and cherish them as the lovely myths that they are, the attesting poetry of the zealous, but let us be honest and simply recognize them for what they are, and know and accept them as such. . . . What the church should be and teach is far too important to be buried and obscured behind the centuries-accumulated wall of its careless and considered droppings.

A person from Vermont

I want to thank you for your two books on the historical Jesus. I have waited for these books ever since I was ten or twelve years old. [Writer is at least eighty-five years old at this time]. . . . You will be interested to know that there are some alert church members who are showing an interest in what you have written and who want to make a serious study of the historical Jesus.

A man from Iowa

The historical Jesus you described provided a new way for our church to think of Him that, if needed, enhances his stature in modern terms. . . . You have stimulated my religious curiosity and sober investigation and I know stimulated others. . . .

A man from Illinois

I have to write you this letter thanking you for works in recent years concerning the "historical Jesus.". . . As a Christian not willing to have a lobotomy, I find your honesty concerning what we really know about Jesus very refreshing. In an age when fundamentalists and their threats have cowed so many scholars from seeking the truth, your works stand out. . . . In fact, I would say that my faith has actually been strengthened by knowing and understanding the context in which Jesus lived and worked.

A man from Illinois

While a student in the 70s I was affiliated with the Catholic Worker movement, which emphasized the radical aspect of the teachings of Jesus. This experience inspired me to a career in geriatrics. I find that the dying are not comforted by the historical Jesus, they are more comforted by the good news proclaimed in its entirety followed by: "This is the word of the Lord." This includes the message . . . that proclaims an "empty tomb" and appearances to women, and Thomas, who was told to physically examine the wounds. If it is not true, then Christianity is a two-thousand-year hoax and fraud. As Paul states: Christians are the most miserable of the miserable if this complete message is poisoned by mythology.

A woman from Florida

I liked your book [Jesus: A Revolutionary Biography] and hope it will contribute to the long-range effect of putting Jesus' message in a more rational framework. It seems to me that your point of view may strengthen the message rather than weaken it—although I must say that over the years (I was raised a Methodist) I have found the whole idea of Jesus' resurrection, at least in the traditional sense, and the concept of a "life after death," that is, the idea that my consciousness will somehow survive my death, increasingly difficult to accept—even though I remain interested in religion and fond of my memories of church.

A man from Michigan

Works like yours that discredit Jesus bring accolades and high praise from a secular world but man does not have the last word. I am not a priest or a pastor but a Christian who cannot stand by while such attacks are being waged without speaking up. Remember, Jesus had to knock Saul off his mule and

*temporarily blind him in order to get his attention.
Therefore, I challenge and invite you, in Christian
love, to humble yourself and seek Him, then and
only then will He make Himself known to you as He
did me and you won't have to question His divinity
or His resurrection—you will know—He is risen!!*

A man from West Virginia

*The statement [attributed to Dr. Crossan in the
Chicago Tribune Magazine of July 17, 1994 by
Jeff Lyon] about Jesus not resurrecting from the dead
is absurd. Are you trying to say that after his execution He did not rise from the dead? In other words
you think that he is still dead. Well, as far as I'm
concerned, my Jesus is alive because he lives inside
my heart. I can also see his wonders every day. He
keeps me alive by the air I breathe. He protects me,
feeds me, clothes me, and supplies my needs. So how
dare you say He never resurrected from the dead.
Even the Bible says so.*

A girl from Illinois

What about Easter Sunday?

In discussing the crucifixion, I argued that the
story of Jesus' burial by his friends was totally unhistorical. If he was buried at all, he was buried not by
his friends but by his enemies. And not in a tomb
hewed out of stone, but in a shallow grave that
would have made his body easy prey for scavenging

animals. Those are grim conclusions, but I cannot escape them.

With the Easter stories, are we standing on the solid rock of historical fact? Or, if not, how are we to account for the survival of faith in Jesus? And if we decide that we cannot read the Easter narratives literally, then how *are* we to read them? I raise these questions not just because for some twentieth-century people the notion of resurrection from the dead seems incredible on the face of it. I raise these questions also because the New Testament record forces me to raise them. Matthew, Mark, Luke, and John tell the Easter story quite differently — so differently, in fact, that we simply cannot harmonize their versions. So we have to ask questions of intention and meaning.

In a nutshell, these are my conclusions: First, the Easter story is not about the events of a single day, but reflects the struggle of Jesus' followers over a period of months and years to make sense of both his death and their continuing experience of empowerment by him. Second, stories of the resurrected Jesus appearing to various people are not really about "visions" at all, but are literary fiction prompted by struggles over leadership in the early Church. Third, resurrection is one — but only one — of the metaphors used to express the sense of Jesus' continuing presence with his followers and friends.

So you're saying that the Easter story is just a fairy tale — a sort of Hollywood happy ending.

No, I'm not saying that at all. But you could certainly get that impression if you just read the accounts in the gospels uncritically. You know how the story goes: Friday was tragic, Saturday was desolate, on Sunday the tomb was empty and all was well.

It's perfectly true that Jesus' followers fled when he was taken and executed. And that's entirely understandable. But it's a terrible trivialization to suppose that they all lost their faith on Friday and miraculously got it back on Sunday. I have tremendous respect for those first Christians. I think that, far from losing their faith when Jesus was killed, they kept it alive and even deepened it.

But what about the empty tomb?

Is the story of the empty tomb historical? No. I've already explained why I doubt there was any tomb for Jesus in the first place. I don't think any of Jesus' followers even knew where he was buried—if he was buried at all. And the gospel writers don't come close to agreeing with each other on what they report. So my conviction is that motives other than just history writing are clearly at work here.

By the way, Paul is the earliest writer we have on resurrection—his letters are much earlier than the gospels—and he nowhere shows awareness of having heard an empty tomb story. That's hard to understand, if an empty tomb was supposed to be the bedrock historical fact of Easter.

Well, what are the bedrock historical facts, then?

Let's look for a moment completely outside the records produced by Christians. Are there any "outside" witnesses we can call upon for some help? The answer is yes.

First, there is the Jewish historian I've often referred to, Josephus. Writing near the end of the first century, he describes Jesus as a wise man "who wrought surprising feats," was accused by high-standing Jewish leaders, and put to death by Pilate. But, Josephus adds, "those who had in the first place come to love him did not give up their affection for him," so that "the tribe of the Christians, so called after him, has still to this day not disappeared."

The second witness is the Roman historian Tacitus, writing early in the second century. He mentions that "Christus" had been sentenced to death by the procurator Pontius Pilate. Then, with a sneer, he notes that the "pernicious superstition" of his followers, far from being snuffed out, even found its way to Rome, "where all things horrible or shameful in the world collect and find a vogue."

So we have two outside sources, one neutral in tone and one insulting. But both agree on the outline of what happened. There was a movement over there in the "colony." Its founder was executed by Pilate. But, instead of ending there, as might have been expected, the movement continued, and has now reached Rome itself. Tacitus and Josephus, of course, are not Christians, and don't speak of "resurrection." But they do witness to *unexpected continuity* in the movement connected with Jesus.

That's a long way from resurrection, though.

Perhaps. But maybe resurrection is simply a word-picture of Jesus' continuing presence among his followers.

In the *Gospel of Thomas*, for example, only one title is ever used of Jesus. He is called simply the "Living Jesus." His followers experience him as the Wisdom of God on earth, still present and acting, just as when he was walking around their countryside. Those missionaries we talked about earlier, sent out by Jesus to offer free healing and share open meals in the homes and hamlets of Galilee—do you really think they just dropped everything the day he died? Just immediately all lost their faith? No. I think that they found themselves just as empowered as they had been before. And that meant that somehow Jesus was still with them. So they struggled to find a way to express that powerful and empowering *presence* of Jesus. That way *was* the Easter story.

You talked about Easter as not one day, but a period of months or even years. What do you mean by that?

What I mean is that Jesus' execution forced his followers to wrestle with some very tough questions. How could he have come to such a fate? How could Jesus have suffered a disgraceful death at the hands of imperial authority and still be what their experience persuaded them he was—God's wisdom and power?

You might picture two different groups of Christians. The itinerant missionaries in Galilee worked it out with their hot, sore feet as they walked from house to house continuing his mission. The more scholarly sorts in Jerusalem pored over the texts of their scriptures to understand what had happened. Not because they had *lost* their faith, but because they were trying to *understand* and *explain* how it was that their faith persisted in spite of what had happened.

The Emmaus Road story in Luke 24, mentioned in Chapter 6, is a good example. Think about it not as a single day that you could have caught on your camcorder if you had been there, but as a pictorial summary of the whole rethinking struggle I described above. See if it makes sense to you that way.

In the story, the two itinerant missionaries are going out on Easter Sunday from the Jerusalem community toward Emmaus, seven miles down the road. As they walk, they're deep in sorrow, talking about the terrible events of Jesus' arrest and crucifixion. A stranger joins them and asks what they're discussing. They can't believe he doesn't know what's been happening, and tell him about the execution of Jesus, who was "a prophet mighty in deed and word before God and all the people." And they report the strange tales of women who had found his tomb empty. The stranger rebukes them for being "slow of heart" in believing what the Jewish scriptures say, and asks rhetorically, "Was it not necessary that the Messiah should suffer these things and then enter into his glory?"

But Cleopas and his companion still don't understand who they're talking to. When they approach

Emmaus, the stranger appears intent on going on, but they talk him into staying with them. They go in to eat. Listen to the story:

> *When he was at the table with them, he took bread, blessed and broke it, and gave it to them. Then their eyes were opened, and they recognized him; and he vanished from their sight. They said to each other, "Were not our hearts burning within us while he was talking to us on the road, while he was opening the scriptures to us?"*

That's the story. If you ask me whether it's historical in the sense of being a straightforward account of what happened to two people on Easter Sunday, I say no. But it is *certainly* historical in the sense of describing a *process over time* that happened in the Christian community. That is, they did come to believe that the Living Jesus "opened their minds to understand the scriptures." They did find in their tradition the hints they were looking for that, despite his ignominious death, Jesus was the agent of God's purpose. And he did keep meeting them "in the breaking of the bread." That is, as Christians continued to gather for the open communal meals to which Jesus had introduced them, they experienced him as present. Continuing to empower them for the work of the Kingdom, he was the "Living Jesus."

You might put it this way: the Emmaus story isn't a fact, but it is true. It's a symbolic picture of Christian faith deepening over time. Easter was much, much more than the events of a single day.

Okay, that makes sense. But I still want to go back to the idea of resurrection. After all, that seems to be a central New Testament claim. Right?

Right. I'm saying that resurrection is only one of several ways that Christians could think about their experience of "Jesus-with-us." So the question is where that emphasis on resurrection comes from. And the answer is: from Paul.

If you look at 1 Corinthians 15, you find Paul—and this is twenty to forty years before the gospels were written—defending the idea of bodily resurrection. But here's a very interesting twist: He never argues that resurrection was a special miracle only for Jesus. Just the opposite: Jesus' resurrection is for him one instance of a *general* resurrection.

It's easy to see how he develops his argument. Before his conversion, Paul had been a devout Pharisee—and Pharisees believed that God would raise up the righteous dead at the end of "this present age." Paul, as you know, was on his way to Damascus to persecute Christians when he had an experience that we would call *vision* or *trance*—a blinding light, a voice, a fall to the ground. To Paul, this was an encounter with the Jesus he was attacking. How would he understand this experience of Jesus? I think the answer is that he would conclude that *the general resurrection has begun.* In fact, that's exactly the way he describes his belief: Jesus is "the first fruits of those who have died." Given his expectation of a general resurrection, his experience of Jesus would persuade him that it had in fact begun. Jesus isn't the *only* one to be raised, just the *first*.

It is significant that Paul does not say, "If Christ's tomb is not empty, vain is our faith," but, "if Christ is not risen, vain is our faith." He is not talking about the resuscitation of Jesus' corpse but about the presence of Jesus in a wholly new mode of existence. It is, for Paul, the same Jesus who once was an earthly presence limited by time and place, who now is a transcendant presence unlimited by time and place.

So Paul was wrong about the resurrection?

No, I'm not saying that Paul was wrong. Just that his experience was *his* experience—not everybody else's. But I don't see any reason to believe that *all* of Jesus' followers would have reasoned the same way. After all, most of them were peasants, not Pharisees like Paul with a sophisticated training in interpretation of scripture. And since Paul had been a bitter enemy of the movement, his trance-experience would have been a unique outworking of his own psychological conflict. So I don't see any reason to suppose that either his experience or the way he interpreted it (that is, as a meeting with a resurrected Jesus) was typical of other Christians. As I said before, those peasant followers in Galilee knew Jesus' presence in their sore feet. Those scribes in Jerusalem were meeting him again in their study of scripture. So Paul's use of the category of resurrection was just one possible way of talking about the presence and power of Jesus in the lives of his followers.

In fact, I'd go even further. Paul's image of Jesus as the "first fruits of those who have died" depends upon the notion that the full harvest is at hand. But if that isn't the case, the metaphor doesn't work very well. If Paul were here today, I might ask him, "Paul, we've been waiting a long time since the 'first fruits' for that harvest you talked about. Maybe you weren't quite right about that general resurrection being just around the corner. Is there a better way to talk about Jesus' presence among us than 'resurrection?'"

How do you personally think about it? What is your own Easter faith?

Easter means for me that the divine empowerment which was present in Jesus, but once upon a time limited to those people in Galilee and Judea who had contact with him, is now available to anyone, anywhere in the world, who finds God in Jesus. As far as I'm concerned, it has nothing to do, literally, with a body coming out of a tomb, or a tomb being found empty, or visions, or anything else. All those are dramatic ways of expressing the faith. The heart of resurrection for me is that the power of God is now available through Jesus, unconfined by time or space, to anyone who believes and experiences it.

But what about all the stories of the risen Jesus appearing to people? If Easter for you doesn't have anything to do with visions or a literal

resurrection, what do you do with all those stories?

That's a very important question. Let me tell you what I've concluded, and then give an illustration or two.

We usually regard those stories of post-Easter appearances by Jesus as visions of some sort. I think they're nothing of the kind. They have no marks that you would expect—no blinding lights, no heavenly voices, nobody knocked to the ground. Neither does Jesus bring back from "the other side" some new revelation, as you might expect. Rather, what really matters is *who Jesus appears to*. That is, these stories are dramatizations with a political purpose. And that purpose is to tell us who's in charge, now that Jesus is no longer personally present.

Here's the clearest example. In John 20, you have a story of a race by two disciples to the empty tomb. Peter and the unnamed follower called the Beloved Disciple run toward the tomb. The Beloved Disciple outraces Peter, gets to the tomb, looks in and is the first to see the discarded linen wrappings. Because there was an older tradition that *Peter* had been the first to the tomb, he is allowed in this version to actually *enter* the tomb first. But when the Beloved Disciple next enters the tomb, he alone is said to *see and believe*. Thus he takes first place away from Peter.

But there's more. Next to be subordinated to the Beloved Disciple is Mary Magdalene. In Matthew's gospel (28:8–10) she meets and worships the risen

Jesus. But here in John she fails to recognize Jesus when he appears to her, and three times gives the wrong interpretation of the empty tomb: "They have taken away my Lord." And finally, the Beloved Disciple is exalted over Thomas, whom we have immortalized as "Doubting Thomas." In this story he refuses to believe unless and until he can personally see and touch the wounds from the crucifixion. When Jesus does appear to him, he is rebuked in words that at the same time honor the Beloved Disciple: "Have you believed because you have seen me? Blessed are those who have not seen and yet have come to believe."

Stories like that tell us absolutely nothing of historical value about the origins of Christian faith. But they tell us a great deal about the origins of Christian *authority*. They are competing pictures about who has priority and power in the early Christian community. John 20, for example, tells us that in the community of the Beloved Disciple, Mary Magdalene's authority had to be challenged as much as that of Peter or Thomas. And, of course, we have outside the New Testament a *Gospel of Peter*, a *Gospel of Mary*, and a *Gospel of Thomas*. Stories like this presume a community that has been around for a long time—probably for one or two generations. But they really have nothing to do with appearances on Easter Sunday. They are dramatizations about where power and authority rest in the early Church.

And they're not entirely innocent stories, either. If you read them carefully, you'll find that the trend is

away from Jesus' egalitarian community toward invest-
ing authority either in a leadership group (the Twelve)
or in specific individuals (e.g. Peter or the Beloved
Disciple). Already we're on our way toward a church
led by a male hierarchy. And that's a long way from
where Jesus started.

So the "appearance" stories aren't the historical record of one day—Easter Sunday—right?

That's what I'm arguing, yes. There may well have
been visions, of course. There are always visions in
religion, and Paul certainly had a vision of Jesus. My
point is that those stories in the last chapters of the
gospels are not and were not intended to describe
visions.

Then summarize if you will what we are left with, historically.

What happened historically is that those who
believed in Jesus before his execution *continued* to do
so afterward. Easter is not about the start of a new
faith but the continuation of an old one. Despite his
crucifixion, Jesus was for his followers alive, present,
and empowering them to do the work of the Kingdom
still. That's the only mystery and the only miracle, and
as far as I'm concerned, it's more than enough of both.
Of course, there may have been visions and trances.
There are always such in every religion, and I've no

reason to think that Paul was alone in his. But the basic reality is that those whom Jesus empowered as healers and invited around an open table kept his vision and program alive, and continued to experience his presence in that vision and program. That, to me, is Easter.

Do you personally believe in life after death for us?

First, a little bit of history. In the entire Old Testament until the time of the Maccabees in the second century before Jesus, there is not the slightest hint of belief in an afterlife, even though the whole world around Israel believed it. As far as those scriptures were concerned, God was eternal but people, even God's people, were not. If they had eternal life, it was by being part of God's people because God's people as a community lived on. I've looked at Jewish grave engravings from the second and third centuries of our era, and even then the views are mixed, some with belief in afterlife, some not. So belief in life after death has certainly not always been part of biblical faith.

Second, I think we need to raise a question: Is the primary purpose of God to guarantee our immortality? It would seem to be so for many people to whom, if there is no immortality, there's no sense of even believing in God.

Third, I do think that part of our human need is to create what I call "metaphors of immortality."

That is, we all need something bigger than ourselves
to live for, and something bigger than ourselves to
live on after us. That may be a family, a nation, an
organization, a church, or whatever is authentically and communally greater than our own indi-
viduality. A metaphor of immortality gives life and
death meaning.

Do I personally believe in an afterlife? No, but to
be honest, I do not find it a particularly important
question one way or the other. I am not in the least
bit interested in fighting those who believe or hope
in it. My own interest is in how we live our lives here
below. I am sure that we are called to do the will of
God "on earth, as in heaven." Heaven, however, I
leave up to God. Earth is where our responsibility
lies, that is where the Kingdom of God is lost or
found.

But if we build the meaning of this present life
on its being eternal, I'm pretty sure we're wrong.
Or if we use the prospect of eternal life to dull us to
the present world and its injustices, we're wrong. If
there is not enough meaning in life that we must
imagine having it in a future life, we're wrong. I
think those in earlier generations who painted pictures of hell as well as heaven had it right—they
saw both good and evil in the human story. Their
problem was that they banished heaven and hell to
the *future*. *Our* problem is that we try to believe in
heaven without facing hell. My view is that both
heaven and hell are present here and now. We
make life. We make this world heaven or hell. So
far, and in general, we have made it more hell than

heaven. To put it in biblical terms: either we try to fashion the world in the image of the Kingdom Jesus envisioned, or we abandon it to the world's Caesars and Pilates.

9

How Do You Get from Jesus to Christ?

Earlier tonight my friend came by with his son.
I read him a couple of lines from Crossan
having to do with forms of peasant resistance.
I do not say anything about Jesus to my friend
although he is always more than kind when I do.
In fact, I discuss Jesus more
with my Buddhist friends than I do with Christians.
This is a painful fact. Let me quote one sentence:
"Open commensality has been both ritualized,
which was probably inevitable,
and ruined, which was not."
I have not been a model of faith.
I have been nowhere all night waiting for this book.

A man from Washington

For Dominic: You have provided a framework within which I could say I am a Christian—something I have not been able to say for very many years.

A person from Minnesota

I apologize to you, for the damage I did to you during my undergraduate studies in Christianity. . . . Without so much as having even opened one of your books, [my classmates and I] badgered you and then dismissed you in what we labeled your turpitude. . . . I received the book [Jesus: A Revolutionary Biography] as a present but didn't read it until recently. . . . I believe that you have raised serious questions which demand the soulful attention of all religious people. . . . Your writing bears the mark of aweful, soul-empowering inspiration. You have shown me how to open some doors for myself—to have the courage to question what I know I should question. I will pray for the strength of heart that you've demonstrated in your book.

A man from Virginia

Most United Kingdom clergy, for example, take for granted that Jesus said or did everything that is recorded in the Gospels. Our group finds it increasingly irksome having to endure sermons and lectures which ignore the most elementary conclusions of biblical scholarship. Living with the gap is challenging. On the one hand, it enables us to speak with nonchurchgoing professionals about Jesus and his followers in ways which do not insult their intelligence and integrity. On the other hand, the paradigm shift has such radical consequences for normal church discourse and worship that very few church people can face them. Do you also encounter this gap?

A group from England

You intimated somewhat through your writing that you did not believe historically, and I would venture to say personally, that Jesus was the Son of God, as is accepted in orthodox Christianity. And so I wonder what exactly your impression of modern-day Christianity is? What do you think of the millions of people who believe in a future Kingdom of God based upon the death and resurrection of Jesus, the atonement of mankind's sin through his sacrificial death, and the concept of eternal salvation as being a gift according to the grace of God, do you think that they are all misled and wrong?

A woman from California

Let's suppose your picture of the historical Jesus is right on target. What does that mean for me as a disciple of Jesus? In concrete terms, what would following Jesus look like today? How should Christians live today?

A man from Virginia

It's time for a summing-up. If someone who had never heard of Jesus asks you to tell his story in just two or three minutes, what would you say?

I'd say that Jesus lived in an occupied land, among peasants who had long existed at a subsistence level and were being pressed harder and harder. It was a world of structured inequality and injustice. *In that world*, he offered and lived out an alternative vision.

And he invited others to share it: a community of free healing and shared eating, a community of equals before God and each other. To women, children, men, to lepers, the destitute, the disturbed, he issued the same invitation: Come eat with me and be healed, and take what you experience to others. That new community was what the Kingdom of God looked like, what the whole world would look like if God, not Caesar, were directly in charge. That is what it means for God's will to be done on earth as in heaven.

But "heaven" was in good shape —*earth* was the problem. That's why Jesus didn't just talk about the Kingdom, but *acted it out.* He plowed the vision of the Kingdom into the soil of his own society. That made him a revolutionary figure —not in a military sense, but in a social sense. And he died for his vision of the Kingdom. Though his sharp challenge to the usual arrangements of his world could have gotten him arrested at any time, his symbolic destruction of the Temple provided the immediate excuse for high Jewish and Roman authorities to move against him. And we can hardly even imagine the brutal offhandedness with which a peasant nobody like Jesus would have been crushed in a Jerusalem under the likes of Caiaphas and Pilate.

But what was totally unexpected was that the end of this troublesome Jewish peasant was not the end after all. Those who had originally experienced God's power through their life together with him continued to experience it after his death. Now that power was no longer confined by time or place, but was available anywhere to those who saw God in him. That is why the prudently neutral historian Josephus reported at the end of the first century that "those who had in the first place come to love him, did not give up their affection for him . . . and the tribe of the Christians, so called after him, has still to this day, not disappeared."

Such is my picture of the historical Jesus. In his offer of free healing and common eating he announced and created a community that was his *no* to the established hierarchical, patronal patterns of his society. Lest he himself be interpreted as simply the new broker of a new God, he moved on constantly, never settling down. He would not be a mediator, but rather the announcer that no mediator should exist between persons, or between persons and God. He announced, in other words, the unmediated or broker-less Kingdom of God.

One of your critics has suggested that your emphasis on Jesus as a peasant resister in an imperial colony comes out of your own experience of growing up in Ireland under British rule. Is that possible?

Well, it's certainly true of all of us that what we see depends on where we stand when we look. If you are a woman in a male-dominated society, or an African-American in a white-dominated society, for example, you may indeed see realities that others either miss or deny. And in that sense, no doubt I grew up unlikely to see empire as a benign reality. But

if so, I'd say that my life experience led me to *see*
something that was really going on with and around
Jesus—not to *invent* it.

I grew up among the first generation of post-
colonial Irish as the British Empire was beginning
to decline. I certainly learned what awful things
Britain had done to Ireland—but I also received a
classically British education, including texts chosen to
prepare British youths to administer the Empire. And
while my paternal grandparents were lower class peasant farmers, my maternal grandparents were middle
class urban shopkeepers. I repeat: I hope that my background sensitized me to injustice, in the first century
as well as the twentieth, but I deny that it moved me
to invent first-century evidence that wasn't really
there.

*The Jesus you reconstruct—moving among peas-
ants to rebuild society "from the bottom up"—
sounds a lot like the Jesus of Latin America's
liberation theology.*

If so, it's not because I am a student of liberation
theology. If the historical Jesus fits into the Latin
American situation, perhaps it is because that situation actually resembles his.

Think, for example, of Archbishop Oscar Romero.
In the late 1970s he became Archbishop of San
Salvador, in a land where a tiny wealthy elite con-
trolled politics, economics, and the military while the
vast majority lived in peasant poverty. Historically, the

Church had identified with the interests of the elite. But Romero, as a good pastor, went out among the people—and the people converted their bishop. He began to speak out forcefully, both against unjust privilege and violence on the political right, and against violence and ideology on the guerrilla left.

Against those who wanted a gospel "so disembodied that it doesn't get involved at all in the world it must save," he insisted that "God is doing *now*" what Christ did *then*: "shaking off oppressive yokes, bringing joy to hearts, sowing hope." He became the voice for the voiceless: those in shacks and shanty towns, coffee harvesters, the "disappeared" and tortured. Only the person who is concerned for the hungry, the naked, the poor, the tortured, he said, "has God close at hand." Mere charity, he insisted, is not enough, for it is "a caricature of love to try to cover over with alms what is lacking in justice." In the words of his Christmas Eve homily in 1979:

> *We must not seek the child Jesus in the pretty figures of our Christmas cribs.*
> *We must seek him among the undernourished children who have gone to bed tonight without eating, among the poor newsboys who will sleep covered with newspapers in doorways.*

Accused by politicians and media of supporting subversion, he denied the charge—"unless the gospel is to be called subversive, because it does indeed touch the foundations of an order that should not exist, because it is unjust."

Predictably—and he was aware of the fate awaiting him—Archbishop Romero was murdered by a death squad while saying Mass, in Lent, 1980.

But, like the Jesus story, it didn't end there. When, thirteen years later, a group of scholars gathered in Chicago for a symposium on my historical research, I was moved by the reflections of Catherine Keller, who teaches in the Theology School of Drew University. She had recently returned from El Salvador, where she admitted "that for the first time in my life the early Christian story became real for me." There she encountered a grassroots community organized around *eating* (for example, taking food to university students held in prison, and not fed by the government) and *healing* of bodies and psyches.

Though the "resurrected Romero" appeared on murals everywhere, she said, "he appears on a continuum with all the other people's martyrs, male and female, who gave their life for the people—precisely *not* in any grotesque attempt to satisfy God through an atoning sacrifice, but by sharing their lives so fully that the death forces could not tolerate them." She found people living boldly in the face of death—with "zest and high good humor, a delight in the sensuality of terrestrial life, an iridescent hope (not optimism), combining itself with clear critical analysis of history and global politics." In such community, she said, she felt close to what Jesus called the Kingdom of God. Crucifixion and resurrection became present realities for Keller through one Salvadoran woman's sense of the legacy of her mother, who had been abducted, raped, and murdered because of her commitment to justice: "The evil forces were not able to stop what for her had meant life."

Who can hear such a story and not recognize in our own generation the continuing reality and power of the gospel of the Kingdom?

Your picture of the historical Jesus—how does it fit with Church teachings about him?

The question deserves a book of its own! But let me try to put it in a nutshell. Our term "Jesus Christ" sums up the issue. "Jesus" is the historical person; "Christ" affirms who he is for believers. "Christ" comes from a Greek word which means the same as "Messiah" which comes from a Hebrew word. Both mean "the Anointed One" and they sum up Jewish hopes for a God-sent deliverer. "Jesus Christ" is thus not a first and last name, but a name and a title: "Jesus who is the Christ (Messiah)."

Christian faith is always *faith in the historical Jesus as a manifestation of God to us.* Faith is more than historical reconstruction. Someone might think that I had done a good job of scholarly research and say, "That's all very interesting, about Jesus' itinerancy, his challenge to conventional lifestyle, his open meals . . . but nothing I want to organize my life around." It's possible to accept the historical facts but to conclude that Jesus was utopian, or mistaken, or flaky, or whatever. Christian *faith* means finding in the picture of the historical Jesus the power and wisdom of God—and then getting serious about its implications for *our* lives, now.

So faith goes beyond the historical *facts* to wrestle with their *meanings*. But faith cannot ignore or bypass the historical facts. What we believe in by faith is the ultimate meaning of what we know by history. But the historical reconstruction informs the faith. If I find, for instance, that the historical Jesus called people into an "unbrokered" relationship with God, I can't very well put my faith in a Christ who is conceived as the sole mediator between God and humanity. If I find a Jesus who acts out the Kingdom around an open table, I can't invest faith in a Christ who is a social or moral segregationist. "Christ" is more than "Jesus," but not less. In short, if my faith in Christ doesn't interpret at the deepest level what I know about the historical Jesus, I'd better reexamine my faith.

Your books make a lot of sense to me, but I have a problem of sitting through church on Sunday and having lots of questions in my mind about what is going on. I find meaning in being part of the Church, but I also don't know what to make of this new way of understanding Jesus. What am I to do?

Well, some elements in any parish may, in fact, need to be reformed. If, for example, one has an authoritarian pastor, then I would say that is unacceptable. I

don't see how there can be argument on that point—
Jesus makes it plain that masters are to behave like
servants. He makes it plain that you can't be a
Christian leader by playing boss. So I wouldn't have
any patience with that kind of parish life.

As for the Eucharist, I would say that its meaning
is that God and Jesus are present to us, as food, but
equally for all. Nobody gets a bigger host or more
wine than another, even in this ritualized form of a
meal. The question is whether our present forms
show some continuity with what Jesus was doing in
his ministry. For me the sense of equality before God
in the community of faith is absolutely central.
Without that sense of equality the tie between Jesus'
meal practice and the Eucharist is broken. So the
critical question is: In our current forms of church
life does our celebration reflect or break continuity
with Jesus?

By the way, what I say about Eucharistic liturgy I
would say also about a Pentecostal celebration.
Take, for example, speaking in tongues. If worshipers
draw the conclusion that those who speak in
tongues are superior to others, that breaks the continuity with Jesus. If they draw the conclusion that
the Spirit is equally available to all and is unpre-
dictable, then they are in continuity with Jesus.
That's the question about our forms, not whether
they are exactly what Jesus did, but whether or not
they are consistent with his basic emphasis. I would
also ask: Is what we do in worship a once-a-week
escape from the world, or is it a beachhead for Jesus'
incursion into the world?

*Will you say something about your own spiritual
life and connection with the Church?*

    I spent twenty years of my life in a monastic
order with four or five hours a day of formal prayer.
I left the priesthood in 1969 because, as I indicated
earlier, I wanted to marry, and also because of an
acute distaste for how the Roman Catholic hierarchy operated. My intelligence and my conscience
were repeatedly insulted, and I was constantly in
trouble for saying out loud what I had found in my
research. I wanted to get away from that. I didn't
want to have to constantly argue with the hierarchy
and let them set my agenda. So I basically decided,
"You leave me alone, and I'll leave you alone." But I
have always considered myself a member of the
Roman Catholic tradition and the Roman Catholic
community. I just need a certain therapeutic dis-
tance, a certain strategic separation from the
Roman Catholic hierarchy. But I would also say
that I can no longer distinguish between prayer and
study. If the function of prayer is to allow God to
get at you, then scholarship is where that now happens for me. Someone asked me in an interview
what I would do differently if I had my life to live
over. I would do it exactly the same way over again,
because I like the way it came out. If I had to do it
all over again, I would spend twenty years in a
monastery. If I had to do it all over again, I would
also leave that monastery.

*If you could wave a magic wand over the Church
to produce any change that you wanted, what
would it be?*

I would reverse the entire method of decision
making so that issues would be decided from the bottom up. I would want a church where there were *no
magic wands* that anybody could wave from the top
down. You know, if the Pope would say tomorrow that
women can now be priests, I'm not at all sure that
would be a good idea—simply because it would be
pronounced from the top down. The world has
changed from an authoritarian, hierarchical style of
public life, and the Church never did change. Even
the *language* has not changed since the time of the
Roman Empire. When I was a monk in Rome, the
allowance that I received for my living expenses was
called by a Latin term that came down from what the
Romans paid the slaves. What I think we need in the
Church is to generate maximum discussion about
important issues, like birth control and abortion,
instead of telling everyone what to think and do. So
if I could wave a magic wand, I would get rid of the
waving of magic wands.

*My final query is a question about a question. If
you got to ask Jesus one question, what would that
question be?*

One of the people who wrote to me did so under
the guise of two letters to Jesus. I cannot think of any

better questions to ask Jesus than the ones formulated in those letters. Here is a combined extract:

Dear Jesus,

A small group of us have just begun reading your biography by Dominic Crossan. At the rate we have started, we may never finish even his shorter version. One of the things Mr. Crossan does at the very beginning of this book is talk about your world, the world into which you came. His point, I believe, is that if we are to truly understand you we must try to know your context. (I've cheated and read ahead.) . . .

So very many of the issues seem different. I am part of a group that has political power, you were not. I can foster changes in the laws, you could not. I can help them be fairer or less fair, you could not. . . . I know it's imperfect, but I just can't believe you would have walked away from it. It can help people. Good laws, at their very best, are loving. I thought that was what we were all about. . . .

You seemed more than other great religious leaders to care about the lives of actual people, their pain, illness, grief. If we are to live life lovingly, does that not mean we are to use whatever loving tools we have to open the possibility for others? Does that hold for you as well? . . .

Is it possible that the words you were speaking then are irrelevant to me in my situation? I cannot believe the intent, to be loving to one another, is outdated. . . .

I am increasingly afraid that in many cases you said exactly what you meant, instead of the

watered-down version I have often chosen to swal-
low. Dr. Crossan has about convinced me that
when you said, "Blessed are the poor, for they are
the only ones who do not have dirty hands," you
meant exactly that. This is a message which is neither comfortable nor palatable, and it is just one of
many. What makes all this far worse is that Dr.
Crossan is one of your followers who, at least in
terms of biology, sees you as a man, conforming to
the laws of physics as other men. Far from
decreasing your status, in my mind at least, it
increases it. It means that without any help from
an E.T., an individual can live as you did and perhaps even die as you died. These are not comfortable thoughts. . . .

I have decided to ask three questions: (1) What
were you advocating as a life program in your time
and place? (Crossan is a great help in this, some of
the first I have received that seems sensible); (2)
How does that message translate to me and to today?
(Crossan is helpful here, but he could do more in this
respect . . . another book perhaps?); (3) When I
can answer number two above, passably well, I will
ask: Do I agree with you? Can I do it—or, perhaps
more honestly, am I willing to?

I have a terrible feeling that I may find my
answers most uncomfortable. However, I believe I
would rather say, "I think you were wrong" (however blasphemous that may sound) than try to
fudge it all by maintaining you didn't actually say
it. I also think I will be more at peace with myself
(although not very) saying, "I can't do as you ask"

than I will be if I am a hypocrite about what it is that you have asked. It seems to me that the weak fared better than the hypocrites when you were teaching. . . .

A woman from Ohio

JOHN DOMINIC CROSSAN is emeritus professor of biblical studies at DePaul University in Chicago. He is the best-selling author of many books, including *The Historical Jesus*, *Jesus: A Revolutionary Biography*, *The Essential Jesus*, and *Who Killed Jesus?*

Chapter

The idea of mummifying Jacqui and giving her a tomb didn't come to me right away. Ideas like that have to filter into your mind gradually. It was weeks after the party before I began to have it clear.

It was first triggered by an article I read in the paper about builders somewhere in the States who discovered a mummufied woman in an old house. They were doing alterations, and they broke into a secret room where someone had put her, years before.

Then, another day, I saw all these tombs in Westminster Abbey. I'd never been in there before. You know how it is, when you live in a place you never go near the sights?

But I had a day's work taking an Aussie couple around London, and they just vanished in the abbey for ages. I got really worried, waiting outside for them with the car. I thought they must have had an accident. (They were well on in years, and he'd been telling me he'd had a heart attack.) Finally, I went in to look for them.

The parking guy outside said I could leave the car for five minutes, so I dived in, and there were these tombs all over the place, with statues on top of them of the people inside.

They were really beautiful. That was so much better than shoving people in holes in the ground, and I thought, "That's a really civilized way to bury someone, in the warm and dry. That's a really nice thing to do for someone you love."

There were those things, and things I'd read about ancient Egypt when I was a kid. Ancient Egypt was one of old Mr. Williamson's interests. He had a big section of books on it in his library, and I used to look at them a lot when I was younger. I think it was more the building side of things he'd studied himself—he was a mason—but there was a lot about death and religion in them, too.

The ancient Egyptians always treated their dead nicely, they never just dumped them or burned them.

Putting Jacqui in a tomb would be the best thing I could do for her. In a tomb she'd be safe and properly looked after.

What I would have liked to do was build her a little sanctuary down at the bottom of the garden. There was tons of room out there, but you could just see the council giving permission.

I'd have built it out of yellow stone like the Egyptian tombs, and I'd have given it a big bronze door. And inside I'd have painted it all with scenes from Jacqui's life.

Not the slagging around bits, of course, you always try and forget the grotty things when people die. But I could have had a big picture of the Cortina, for instance, with her learning to drive. I think she would have liked that.

I'd have done another wall with pictures of that day out we had on the river. The inn would look really good, with the river and all the boats.

A place like that would make you feel better about death. If someone you loved died, you could just go down the garden and there they'd be, all quiet and peaceful in a really clean, pretty little tomb, being looked after and cared for.

But most people would never do something like that, it's too sensible.

And it would get me into trouble. It would be the first thing the police would notice. I had to put Jacqui somewhere no one would ever find her. It had to be somewhere right under their noses, but where no one would ever notice. I saw a movie once where the killer casts the dead woman inside a bronze statue and leaves her in the sitting room, for everyone to see. The statue's of herself, even, so he's really pulling everyone's leg. When people come looking for her, to see what he's done to her, he says, "She *was* a beautiful woman, wasn't she?" and he goes over to the statue and strokes its face and holds its hand and everything. And all the time, the woman they're looking for is right under their noses, only an eighth of an inch away, inside a bronze casting.

I needed something like that. I was looking in the mirror one morning, just making sure I was tidy before I went out to work, when I realized where I had to put Jacqui so she'd be safe and come to no harm. I'd go one better even than bronze. I'd hide Jacqui behind a sheet of glass. The sheet of glass I'd hide her behind was the big mirror over the mantlepiece in the back sitting room.

When you look in a big mirror, you see a whole other room on the other side. If you stand and look at it long enough you think, "I could live in there, if only I could get in past the glass."

That's how it occurred to me that behind the mirror was a great big empty chimney breast, a sort of secret room. That's what a chimney breast is, really, a sort of room within a room where you have a fire. In the castle down in Kent where I took Jacqui, half a dozen people could stand up and walk around in the fireplace.

Mine wasn't quite as big as that, but it was plenty big enough. When I measured it, it was nearly ten feet wide, and it went back to a depth of well over four feet. If I shut off the hearth and blocked up the chimney opening, it would make the perfect place for Jacqui, hidden behind the mirror in a tomb where she'd be safe forever.

Chapter

11

The first thing I did was climb on the roof and put a metal cap on the chimney, to keep out any rain or starlings or things. I had a job finding which pot it was. There was a massive great chimney stack up there with six great big pots about fifty feet off the ground. I had to put up a sixty-foot ladder just to get to them. I found the right chimney by lighting a fire in the grate. I put the metal lid over the pot with the warm air coming out.

Then I set about making a room in the chimney breast. First I took out all the flue bricks up to seven feet high and supported the stack on two lintels. I cut a door through the right-hand side of the breast, so I could get inside it. It was all oak paneling there, so I made the door a hidden one, with a secret catch. It's very easy to make a door in oak paneling so no one can detect it. There was one in the chapel of that castle I took Jacqui to. They used to hide priests there when there was a price on their heads and people used to go around killing them. That was in the good old days.

I bricked up the fireplace and plastered it over to match the rest of the wall, then fitted in an electric fire that had been kicking around at the top of the house for years. It was one of those antique-type electric fires with lumps of colored glass and a cast frame that looked like pewter, very homey and attractive.

I roofed over the opening seven feet up with timber and made a plasterboard ceiling. Then I plastered all the walls up nicely and laid a cement floor.

I tried to decorate it the way Jacqui would have liked it. I left the ceiling white and covered it with two-inch thick polystyrene slabs, so it would be well insulated. Jacqui always liked things classy, so I finished the ceiling off with coping all around and a fancy molding in the middle. The walls I did in a Regency flocked paper, white and gold, and I covered the cement floor with a bit of dark green carpet.

When I'd finished it looked really beautiful. There was this very small room, only the width of a double bed, but really clean and cozy to look at. You felt you could have lived there yourself, it was so nice. I took a wire through the wall, under the floorboards where no one would see it, so there was a light in there.

From the outside you couldn't see a thing. It just looked like an ordinary big chimney breast in an ordinary big house, with the fireplace closed off and an electric fire set in it.

I made the coffin for her myself, too. I didn't buy one of those great big ugly things most people take their last ride in, with big brass handles like the doorknockers on the Hammer House of Horrors.

I made her coffin out of half-inch mahogany boards. It was really beautiful, it was so light and it had such a lovely color. I rubbed the wood down with fine sandpaper till it was like silk, then gave it four coats of marine varnish. When I was done, it had a gloss on it like a millionaire's yacht.

I finished the top off with a sheet of plate glass, set into a groove all the way around, with ground edges and a little ring handle fixed at one end so you could lift it out if you ever needed to.

That way you could see Jacqui just by going in the room and turning on the light. I had an idea that she could see out, too. Anyway, it seemed nicer for her to have a glass lid on her coffin than a solid wooden one. There's something awful about being locked in a box, all screwed down and shut in.

Even ordinary people are scared of that. They put clauses in their wills saying they want metal rods driven through their hearts before they're buried, in case they're buried alive.

It must be the worst thing in the world to wake up in your box and hear the last shovelful of earth smacking down six feet above you and the footsteps of the mourners walking away.

At least Jacqui would always have an open door.

The hardest bit was dealing with the body. I kept putting that off for weeks. I knew I'd have to do it sometime, but I kept shying away. I had half an idea I could maybe rig up Jacqui's tomb with ammonia pipes, and turn it into a cold room, and just have her in a sort of bigger deep freeze.

But you'd never feel safe like that. You'd be at the mercy of every power cut, and you'd never be sure the pump wasn't going to break down. That would be a disaster. Poor Jacqui would go completely rotten.

I passed a butcher shop once where the freezer had broken down, and the stench was terrible. The butcher had been away on holiday, and he was hauling all these putrid carcasses out of the shop. It really was vile.

That would be a terrible thing to risk having happen to Jacqui.

She would need to be embalmed. I finally realized that. The only way she'd be safe was by being turned into a mummy.

I read all the books I could find on ancient Egypt and how they looked after dead bodies. It was amazing what they did all those thousands of years ago.

They used to start off by taking all the soft parts out of the body. They took out all the guts, for instance, and put them in jars which they buried beside the body in the tomb. They took the brain out of the skull by fishing up the nose for it with a hook. They took the eyes out, too, and put artificial ones in the sockets.

I went and spent a day at the British Museum, too. They've got masses of mummies in their Egyptian room. They're all dark and dingy of course, but that's because they're thousands of years old and all faded and dirty. They must have been really beautiful when they were new, all snowy white bandages and bright pictures.

The guard there was very helpful. He knew a tremendous amount about the process. He'd worked there seven years. He was a really nice bloke. He'd been a soldier in the Guards during the war and he showed me all sorts of interesting things I would have missed otherwise.

Like, he showed me a map of the way through Hell in one of the coffins. The Egyptians reckoned that in order to get to Heaven, you had to pass through Hell, so when you died you'd need a map. That's why they painted the map of Hell inside your coffin, to stop you taking the wrong turning and getting lost.

He showed me all the mummification processes, too. How they padded out the bodies with wads of bandages after they'd taken the soft parts out, how they did the whole process.

After my visit to the museum, I was able to make out a shopping list of the things I'd need: A few really sharp knives, a wire hook to get the brain out, a whole great big box of bandages, and about a hundredweight of natron. I phoned all sorts of chemical works before I found the natron. Nowadays it's called "sesquicarbonate of soda." It dries flesh and stops it going rotten.

When I had all the things I needed for the job, I got started on Jacqui.

It was a funny feeling, delving into Jacqui's body. You

see thousands of bodies every day of your life, you push up against them in town, you stand in queues with them in restaurants.

But you never see the inside of one, only the outside. Most people go right through their lives and never see the inside part of another human being.

People are funny like that, they hardly ever want to know about the insides of anything. You see them using things all over the place every day, cars, radios, TVs, calculators, phones, but hardly anyone's ever interested in what makes the things tick. They get nervous, in fact, if you show them the works of anything.

They prefer everything covered up, they shove cowlings and casings all over everything. They sit and stare at a TV tube for years of their lives, but not one in ten thousand ever even wonders what's back of the picture they can see. They'll drive their cars around and rev up and beep their horns, and hardly one of them has any idea how the machine works. They don't even understand the principle of the spark plug.

They can't stand their own thoughts either, or the truth about life. You hardly ever meet anyone in life who is capable of lifting up the bonnet and seeing his own works. It scares people somehow. Life scares them too. They get so they can't look at it straight or see it for what it is.

We're brought up from childhood to hide the truth about ourselves from ourselves.

Your modern man is trained so he never thinks seriously about anything serious. Women will sit around for hours discussing teething and potty training, but they never ask themselves what happens to their child's immortal soul. Men will chatter on all day about football and cricket, but they never ask themselves what they're doing on earth and where they'll be going when their time here is over.

If you bring up the subject, they say stupid things like "When you're dead, you're dead!" As if anyone could possibly *know*.

The Egyptians had a lot more savvy about those things. They certainly thought a lot more seriously about them than we do. They knew the body had an inside as well as an outside. They thought that if your body was destroyed, your soul was lost forever, but if your body could be kept from rotting, then one day your soul would come back to you and you'd be reborn into a better life. So they used to take tremendous care over preserving the bodies.

The books I read were full of pictures of people who'd been dead for thousands of years. They didn't look very nice, really. They were as black as coal, and their faces were all sunk in. But they looked terrific considering their age. I mean, what's going to be left, in four thousand years' time, of the people alive today? Bugger all, that's what. All the people alive today will just vanish off the face of the earth. There won't even be dust left of them.

There'll be millions and millions of them buried. The parsons and priests will all talk about everlasting life and the Resurrection. But four thousand years from now, if you put them all together, there won't be enough of them left to fill a matchbox.

Because no one takes any care of the body anymore.

As soon as you're dead they either fry you to ashes or drop you in a hole in the ground. If it's the fire, you're done for right away. If it's the ground, you last a couple of months longer. The wet and the worms get you soon enough.

Ask any gravedigger and he'll tell you most coffins don't last a twelvemonth. They're only made of chipboard.

I got talking to one of the lads in the graveyard on one of my funeral jobs once (in between the racing form and the handouts), and he told me about an exhumation he did. The woman had been buried less than a year, and he said the coffin was so rotten he fell through the lid. When they tried to lift the box with tackle, it fell to bits. The woman inside was hardly there, just a few bones and a terrible stink. They were all choking over it.

After that, when he saw people visiting graves, it used to make him laugh. There was nothing under the ground to visit. They might as well have laid their flowers in the local park or on the main road, for all the good it did.

It seems to me like the best place of all might be the manhole of a main drain. There's probably as much of your loved one there as anywhere else. A bloody farce like that is the best human society can do nowadays.

One of the books I read had a lot of letters in it written by ordinary Egyptian people, and one of them was from a young wife to her husband. He'd been called up to fight the Jews, who were starting a war somewhere. (Life doesn't change much, does it? Thousands of years later the Jews and the Egyptians are still fighting one another.)

Well anyway, this young wife was very worried about her husband, and she asked him to have his body tattooed with his name and address, so if he was killed in battle someone would send his body home to her to have it embalmed. Otherwise, she said, his body might get lost, and then his soul would be lost forever, too.

That struck me as really very loving and nice. You couldn't imagine anyone being that loving these days. When a man drops dead now, all his wife's interested in is the insurance papers. The rag-and-bone man can have the rest.

I think the Egyptians were right in their beliefs, or at least much more right than people are today. They certainly should have been, they had miles more experience with dead people than we have. That was something they were really into. They treasured their dead, loved them and looked after them, spent millions on building tombs and pyramids for them.

But people today, they're not interested. They can't get rid of dead bodies fast enough. They've got them in the ground almost before they've stopped twitching, and there's got to be a Second Coming or a television strike before they'll ever go and visit the cemetery.

I'm as bad as anyone. If I get down to my own mother's grave once a year, I'm really pushing it. It's just that it's such a drag, driving right across town, and it's usually raining, and then there's nothing left under the ground anyway. There's nothing I'd like better than to have my mother's tomb just out in the garden. I'm sure she'd like it better too.

But nobody asked her what she'd prefer. No one ever asks themselves how the person feels who's being buried. They'd say you were mad if you said the dead felt anything.

They think they're telling the absolute truth, when all it is, is the fashionable way of thinking at the moment. What people think is like what people wear, it's there because it's in the fashion. People change from narrow-bottomed trousers to flares, and they change their ideas of what life's all about at the same time. In fifty years' time, the world's going to have a totally new set of fashions, so how could what people believe nowadays possibly be the truth?

The ancient Egyptians, they believed that only your body died at first. Your soul, the part of yourself you think with, went on living for as long as your body was still intact. Inside your dead body, you were still alive. It was only your organs of communication that were paralyzed by death; your voice, your eyes, your hands. You were exactly the person you were before, except you couldn't tell anyone about it.

When I'd look at Jacqui's body I could really feel how true all that was. Death hadn't changed her a bit. Everyone tells you that when someone dies, the soul goes out of them and they become something completely different, just a lump of clay. But Jacqui didn't change at all. Lying there dead, she looked exactly as she always had when she was lying on her back in bed, miles away in her mind. Which means her soul must have still been in her.

It's the obvious thing, really, the soul staying with the

body. If you talk about it going away, then you have to invent places for it to go to. Churches have invented Heaven and Hell, Purgatory and Limbo, and some people reckon it sort of goes into outer space and just wanders around there listening to people on earth knocking on tables.

But the feeling I got with Jacqui was, your soul doesn't leave your body at all. It lives there or it dies there. When your body's gone, completely disappeared, then your soul dies and disappears as well. While your body is still in one piece, your soul stays in it and stays alive. If you put a body in the ground to rot, then the soul lives as long as the body's there, a year or two. You go into a cemetery where there's a fresh burial, and you can *feel* the soul of the dead person still there, still feeling and thinking. But you go into a really old cemetery, where all the people have been buried a long time, there aren't any souls left anymore, they're all dead. All the bodies under the ground have turned to nothing, and the souls of the people have all perished. There's nothing left of them any more.

That's why really old cemeteries feel so peaceful, why you can relax in them. You can't relax in a new cemetery. It's a sad place and makes you think of sad things all the time. That's on account of all the souls in the ground, dying there, and not wanting to die, and all kind of talking to you and telling you sad things.

But in an old cemetery you can feel really peaceful. You can scratch the moss off the tombstones to read the names, and all you can think of is how beautiful the trees are, and wonder where the blackbird has his nest with his chicks.

It didn't scare me, knowing Jacqui's soul was still safely inside her body, she didn't haunt me or anything. I think when your body dies, the worst part of what you do when you're alive disappears, and only the good bits are left. All the nasty things Jacqui had done seemed to die with her, and her soul was just gentle and quiet. Even someone like Hitler's soul would be like that. Hitler's soul would be like a little child, needing someone to look after it and be kind to it. When we die, we'll all need someone to look after our souls and be kind to them. Unless our bodies are destroyed, and then our souls will be dead anyway.

I hadn't treated her so very badly. I'd killed her, but then we've all got to die. That's inevitable. I hadn't done anything to her that wasn't going to happen to her sometime anyway. But I hadn't killed her soul. That's something that *doesn't* have to happen.

The more I read about the old Egyptian religion, the more it seemed so sensible and nice. You wonder why it ever died out. According to the books, it was destroyed by the Christians. When the Christians got to be top dog, they went around smashing up all the Egyptian temples and killing the priests. They smashed up all the other religions, too, all the temples to Diana and Apollo and things like that. Every country from North Africa to England was covered by little temples in sacred groves, but the Christians broke them up and put their own religion in place of all the others. I suppose most of the people wanted to keep their little churches (after all, it was they who built them), but they weren't allowed to. The people in charge came along and smashed up their statues of the gods and put statues of Jesus and Mary in their places.

They did some really evil and cruel things. There was one story I read, about this beautiful pagan woman in Alexandria the Christians killed by scraping her to death with razor-sharp seashells. She was supposed to be one of the most beautiful and intelligent women who ever lived, but the Christians murdered her because she wasn't one of them. They dragged her from her chariot and butchered her in the middle of the road. They were sent to do it by the Christian bishop, Cyril. Now he's Saint Cyril of Alexandria. It's no wonder we've got such evil laws in this country now, when our religion started with people like him.

Chapter

The first thing I had to do was thaw Jacqui out. When she came out of the freezer, she was as hard as a piece of wood. I left the sheets wrapped around her and laid her on a plank bench I'd set up in the little room in the chimney breast. I kept her in that room all the time. I never got careless and left her outside where anyone could find her. I left her for two days to thaw out, resting on a blanket to soak up any water there might be around, and then got ready to operate on her. I took time off work so I could do it all in one go. I made out I was taking a private party down to Bournemouth for a couple of days, so no one would go asking for me or ringing me up. Then

I disconnected the phone wires and started to embalm her.

So I wouldn't have to hurry, I switched off the central heating in the back sitting room. The weather outside was just above a frost, and it soon got really cold in there, so you could see your breath on the air. Jacqui would keep for days in an atmosphere like that, but without freezing rock hard again.

It was a peculiar feeling, unwrapping her for the first time in nearly twelve months. Her face looked calm and still. She hadn't gone horrible or anything. She looked as if she'd just closed her eyes for a minute. She'd had this blank way of looking, as though she wasn't really thinking anything, as though she was giving her brain a rest. I almost thought she was going to open her eyes any second and say something to me. I thought it might be something kind and considerate, like I was the only one who seemed to give her a thought these days. I sort of waited for her to open her eyes and say it, but of course she didn't.

I was surprised to see she was wearing her nightie, I'd forgotten about that. And I'd forgotten putting her things under her body, her handbag and her elephant-foot jeans, her shortie pullover, her sheepskin jacket and her too-tight shoes.

Of course, they were all miles out of date now. In less than twelve months the fashion had gone over to straight-legged jeans and big floppy sweaters. Poor old Jacqui was behind in the fashions and couldn't do a thing about it.

I didn't put those things back with her, I'd never liked

them. I just made a parcel of them and left them in a corner of the room where they couldn't be seen.

When I'd finished Jacqui off, I dressed her up again in her special clothes. They were easy things to get onto a mummy, and she looked quite nice in them.

I thought of taking a photo of her and suggesting to her family to use it to make up a missing person's poster. That way, pictures of Jacqui looking so lovely and ladylike would be seen by thousands. But I didn't want to get involved with those people again for anything, I decided. Realizing that only I would be seeing her like this, I looked at her for a long, long time. I felt proud of what I'd been able to do for her. To tell you the truth, looking at her that sweet and peaceful, I felt better than I had in a long time.

Until I realized I might just be stalling about getting started with the real work. It would have been so much easier in ancient Egypt. They had Houses of the Dead everywhere who you paid to have this kind of work done for you. If someone died in your house, you let the House of the Dead know and they came around and picked up the body. Then, after a while, they delivered it back to you wrapped up in snowy white bandages and laid out in a wooden coffin, all painted on and cheerful looking. They had beautiful ideas like that. No one can avoid death, it happens to you whether you want it or not. But the Egyptians managed to make it more beautiful than anyone else I ever heard of. In some ways, people today live like pigs compared with how they used to.

The first thing they used to do was sort of filet the body. It would be much easier if you could just put it away whole, but it doesn't work that way. All the soft bits inside your body go rotten very easily, in a couple of hours if you don't watch it. If you have a fresh-killed rabbit, for instance, you've got to get the insides out as soon as it stops kicking, or else the meat isn't fit to eat. It's the same with your lamb chops and beefburgers. At the slaughter-house they cut the animal's throat, and they've got his guts out before he hits the ground. And it's the same with human beings: if you haven't got the body frozen, you've got to take the insides out quick.

The ancient Egyptians used to cut you open down your left side, so it was easy to hide the scar. If you cut someone open down the middle of their stomach, it would be very messy. The edges of the cut would flop about and gape open like a big mouth. But if you cut someone down the side it's sort of hidden, and it closes up from its own weight so you can hardly see a thing. To make it even tidier, the Egyptians used to put a metal plate over the spot. They even engraved it.

It was the hardest thing, really, getting started. It's pretty difficult just to stick a knife in a human being and cut them, even if they've been dead for months. You feel it might hurt them. You sort of expect blood to come squirting out, though of course it doesn't. It's just like cutting fat suet really, it doesn't *do* anything.

It was also very sad, that part. You knew you were going to take this whole body and damage it. The only consolation was knowing it was all going back together

236

again. Still, it was a difficult thing to do, even for me, and I'm much less squeamish than most people I ever met. Some people I've heard of faint if they only cut their finger and a drop of blood pops out.

They often enough carry it to the point of being totally ridiculous. I stopped to help out once at an accident where a young lad on a motorbike got himself badly hurt, and the way the people behaved made me sick. He was smashed up outside a row of houses, and everyone came out to the gate to watch. They were shuddering and clutching their throats, but none of the buggers would help the lad. I had to disentangle him from his bike and haul him from under the car that had hit him, all on my own.

I had a job even finding a place to wash my hands after the ambulance came. (I was all gory right up to my elbows, the lad was bleeding that much.) No one wanted to let me into their houses in case they got a bit of blood in their sinks.

To make up for the way they were treating me and the young lad, they couldn't do enough for the old bitch who'd crucified him. *She'd* pulled out of a side turning without looking, and nearly cut him in half. Someone brought an armchair out for her, and someone else a tray of tea. The lad was lying in the road all ripped and torn, with granite chips and bits of glass and metal sticking out of his face and legs, and the old cow who'd caused it was sitting in an armchair on the pavement, sipping tea and talking about the shock to her nerves.

Anyway, I steeled myself and I did what had to be

done. I cut open Jacqui's body and put her insides in a big plastic bin. The Egyptians always put the viscera in a jar alongside the body. They thought that when you came back to life they'd all be put back by the gods. I didn't have a proper vessel, so I bought a home wine-fermenting tub. It was a five-gallon drum with a wide plastic lid that snapped down and sealed off the air. I filled the whole thing up with natron and packed all the bits in everywhere.

It was while I was taking Jacqui's middle out that I found my child. There was a big lump low down in her insides, and I suddenly realized what it must be, so I cut it out very carefully, and it was a little baby boy about the size of your hand. I'd known it was a boy, all along, but I hadn't imagined him so perfect. You could see little tiny nails on his fingers and toes, and he had a little tiny penis and balls.

I stood a long time looking at my little son. When I first pulled him out, he looked purplish and his skin was very soft. And then I thought, "My little boy should have been alive. I should have been able to hold him to me and protect him, to sit by him while he slept and see his eyes open when he woke up."

But I'd never see any of that. I'd never watch him grow up. I'd never buy little clothes for him, or sit him in his bath, or any of the millions of other little things a man does for his children and never even realizes how lucky he is to be doing them.

I sat down and cried for hours when I thought of all that. I really broke down. I couldn't seem to stop. My face was all slobbery, and I could hardly seem to breathe. I thought, "I should hate Jacqui, it was her stupidity that caused him to die. If she hadn't been so sick in the head, he'd still be alive." I felt I wanted to shout at her, to call her a whore, a slut, every dirty name I could think of.

And then I thought how stupid that would be. You can't love a child and hate his mother, no matter what she's done. The child you love is *made* from her. It doesn't matter if she's been going down on half the blokes in the country, if she's the mother of your children, it still doesn't make sense to hate her.

When I got over the crying I looked at Jacqui and the baby for hours. I think I was there most of the night, just staring at them. I remember hearing a blackbird wake up in the garden while it was still quite dark. I was thinking about this new responsibility, about me being a father and having a son.

The first thing I did, funnily enough, was give him a name. The fashion then was for "Jonathan" and "Benjamin." Everyone you met had kids called that. When they're all grown-up, there'll be so many of them mixed together they won't know one from another. They'll have to give them all numbers, like in *Nineteen Eighty-Four.* I didn't want my kid to have a common name like that.

I didn't want him having a flashy one, either. A lot of parents hope their kids are going to be big shots, and they think if they give them a string of names it'll make them look more important. You get families like that in the taxi all the time. They climb in with this great big jammy kid who's just done a job in his nappy, and all the way to their house it's "Percival John Willoughby, don't do this," and "Percival John Willoughby, don't do that."

Jacqui had a great big string of names like that. She was christened "Jacqueline Maria Sonia Elizabeth," and look where it got her.

You should call kids something simple.

You take all the famous people of history. They had really simple names. A lot of them only had the one name, like Napoleon, or Stalin. You couldn't imagine anyone really famous being known by half a dozen names.

I thought a lot about that, and in the end decided to name him "Eddie." Not "Edward" or "Edwin," just "Eddie." I thought of "Ed" first, but people would only tack "ee" on the end if you did that. People always tack "ee" on the end of every name. Even if you call your son "William," everyone says "Willie." With "Eddie," all they could do was shorten it to "Ed," which was the first name I thought of anyway.

Then, when he had a name, I thought of the best way to preserve him. He was so small I wouldn't need to mummify him, I could just put him in a big bottle of spirits and he'd keep forever. There were a lot of big preserving jars in the kitchen which would do fine, and I made a note to get one of them filled up at the pharmacist's with the right stuff. I'd tell him it was for preserving my appendix or something. In the meantime I wrapped little Eddie up very carefully in a soft towel and put him back in the freezer and got on with the business of finishing Jacqui.

I'd done her insides, and now I had to work on her

240

head. The hardest thing about mummifying a body is the head. You've got to do really horrible things with a head before you can make it keep. For a start, you've got to take the eyes out and then the brain. And you can't do it the way they do in a butcher shop, when they're preparing a sheep or a cow or a pig for people to eat. There they just dig the eyes out with a knife, and chop the skull in half with an axe. To prepare a person for being kept forever, you've got to be a lot more careful than that. I wouldn't have considered I'd preserved Jacqui at all if I'd ruined her eyes or split her skull open.

In modern postmortems they cut the top of the skull off [which was absolutely useless]. That would mean messing up all Jacqui's hair and having a row of stitches across her forehead like Frankenstein's monster.

Then there's a way of getting the brains out from underneath, but to do that you've first of all got to cut the head off at the top of the neck.

The ancient Egyptians' way was to pull the brain out with a hook down one nostril. I thought at first that must be some kind of joke. It really seemed impossible to get someone's brain out through their nostril.

But it really does work. If you push something sharp up someone's nose it just goes straight through. There's a thin little bit of bone at the top, but that's no stronger than a bit of tissue paper, and you go straight through into the brain cavity.

The eyes were worse. I wouldn't even want to think about doing that again. Half a dozen times I thought I was going to chicken out and just leave that. Handling someone's insides is easy in comparison. The eyes are sort of the home of the personality. The hardest thing you'll ever do in your life is take someone's eyes out.

It must have been easier for the old embalmers because they didn't know the people they were dealing with. Taking the eyes out of a stranger's head must be much easier than doing it with someone you know.

When I came to Jacqui's eyes, they still had the contact lenses in. They were sort of stuck on the eyeballs really hard. When I had the eyeballs out of their sockets, I thought I'd peel the lenses off with a knife, but in the end I left them where they were.

I had a job thinking how to preserve them after that. I couldn't put eyes in a load of gritty natron in a box, and they'd look really terrible floating around in a glass jar.

What I did in the end was put them in a china preserving jar, so they'd be in preserving fluid but you couldn't see them. Jacqui had brown irises, so I picked a jar with reddish brown flowers on, to match, and when I'd finished everything else I put it in the coffin with Jacqui, just under the corner of the pillow her head was lying on.

I felt really peculiar doing all this. It occurred to me I was doing something that hadn't been done on earth for thousands of years. All those centuries ago, this was a perfectly normal business. You could have gone to ancient Egypt any day of the week and seen this sort of thing going on. It was normal there, a part of their lives, no one thought twice about it. But in our day and age it was something really bizarre. It was the sort of thing you'd put in a horror movie.

If you could put it in a horror movie and show it to the ancient Egyptians, they'd wonder what you were going on about. A picture of modern traffic would probably scare the life out of them, or a nuclear rocket, but not a picture of a body being mummified.

I was at that stage, with Jacqui all cleaned out and ready for embalming, when the doorbell rang.

Chapter

I thought whoever it was out there would go away in a minute. I'd decided in advance to ignore the doorbell if it rang while I was working on Jacqui. I could have disconnected it, but then people can be very rude, and someone hammering on the knocker would be an awful distraction.

Whoever it was didn't go away. They just kept leaning on the bell and after a few minutes of that I started to get fidgety.

You know how it is when a bell keeps on ringing and ringing? you get rattled. You feel you've got to do something about it. You'll climb out of your bath or get out of bed to answer a doorbell or a phone, even though you know it's only going to be something stupid.

I just couldn't carry on working. I ended up leaving Jacqui alone. I made sure the secret door was completely invisible, then I crept out of the back sitting room and stood at the foot of the staircase listening to the bell clanging away in spurts. Every time I thought whoever it was had gone away, it started up again.

I was beginning to sweat. It was a terrible time for someone to come calling.

I'd left Jacqui all grisly in the secret room, and I was standing in the hall wearing this long white coat I'd bought for the job, and it had bloodstains all down the front. What the hell would anyone think if they came in?

It reminded me of that book about the air crash in the Andes. You know, the one where the survivors ate the people who died because there was no food up on the mountain? And when the rescuers turned up, they were absolutely shattered. There were all these bits of bodies lying around in the snow, and the snow was all stained with big gory patches of blood. There were leg bones where they'd cut the muscles off and heads cracked open where they'd eaten the brains. Of course, the survivors didn't notice it, they'd got used to having dismembered corpses all over the place.

I felt like that. I'd got used to having a corpse in the house, but someone coming in fresh would be horrified.

The ringing didn't stop. After five minutes I crept upstairs to see who it was. I went right to the top of the house, to what used to be the servants' attic in the old days. From there you can look right down on the front drive. You can't see someone under the porch, but you can as soon as they leave it to go away.

The bell rang some more, than I heard the scrunch of feet on the gravel. I kept well back from the window, watching the drive. But no one showed. And then the sound of feet stopped and I thought, "Christ! Whoever it is, is going around the back of the house."

I did a lightning-fast creep back down the stairs. I could hear whoever it was outside shaking all the back doors trying to find an open one. Of course, I'd gone around the house locking all the windows and doors before I touched Jacqui. But you know how it is, you always feel as though you've missed something.

By this time, my heart was in my throat. I was imagining all sorts of things. The law back with a search warrant. A hit man hired by Jacqui's dad! Even an ordinary burglar. I could see everything I'd worked for going up in smoke.

I took the Jap sword down off the wall and stood holding it in the middle of the hall. I must have looked like something out of *The Seven Samurai.* I thought, "Whoever it is out there, I'll top him if he breaks in."

But it was all hopeless, really, I knew that. If someone broke a window or forced a door, there'd be a hell of a row from the burglar alarm. There'd be police cars, fire engines, everything.

I could just see this great big fist outside banging right

close to the sensors on the door, and the bell on the front of the house erupting—I could never have talked my way out this time.

And then, whoever it was just went away. I heard footsteps on the gravel again and rushed upstairs, but I was too late. All I saw was the back of someone's coat through the laurels as they disappeared.

I went back to doing Jacqui, but it was hours before my nerves calmed down and I could think straight again.

I found out who the mysterious visitor was a week later, when I had Jacqui packed in natron and drying out.

It was that stupid French bird who was at the party. I came home late one night, and there she was perched on the doorstep waiting for me.

When I got her inside the house, she gave me this big spiel she'd made up. She'd probably worked it out in her French/English dictionary. She made me sit down, then sat opposite me and trotted out this big speech.

"I'ave fall in love wiz you," she said. (She had about as much expression as a clerk in the post office asking you how many stamps you want.) "I love you because you are wurzy of my love. You do not take advantage of me when I am 'elpless—you do not violate my body. Now I zink you merit my body. I give you right to make love wiz me. I come around laz week on my day off to tell you thees, but you are not at 'ome."

You can imagine how I felt listening to all this rubbish. The silly mare had frightened the life out of me, and now she was asking me to screw her, just like that.

I was off birds at that time. Altogether. Even if I'd been on them, I wouldn't have put myself between the sheets with a woman who wasn't right in the head.

But I had to be careful not to offend her. "Hell hath no fury," and all that. I was out all day, and God knows what she'd have done to my place if I'd got her angry. Drug addicts have got about as much sense of responsibility as a bunch of monkeys.

That first night, I told her I'd only nicked back to the house for a bunch of keys, and had to dash back to work again.

She tried to get me to give her a quickie, "To concretize our love," she said.

"Sure," I thought, "that would be a right little cement waistcoat if I got involved with you."

I managed to talk her out of it. I gave her a load of rubbish like, "Something so beautiful shouldn't be hurried." I can't remember exactly how I put her off that first time, I was so furious and boiling up inside with the stupid cow.

I had to waste a lot of time in the next few weeks running around with her in the car. She worked for this glossy little woman who had a couple of fat little kids, and I was always cleaning sticky gunge off the upholstery.

It's terrible when a woman's got a hold on you like that. I felt like murdering her.

Chapter

One day the silly old French cow brought around this bloke to introduce him.

"I am sorree," she said, "but Ricky 'as my 'eart."

"He can have the rest of you, and good riddance," I thought.

You should have seen the state of "Ricky." He had more hair than an Old English sheepdog, and his teeth were so yellow you could have used them for "No Parking" cones.

And his clothes! I felt like shampooing the couch he'd been sitting on. You wouldn't have worn his jeans and jerkin for changing your oil in, you'd have wanted something cleaner.

"Thanks for coming to tell me," I said. "It was very decent of you."

She took Ricky away without realizing that she had saved her life and me a lot of work. I was still busy with Jacqui.

I didn't really know what to do with the natron. No one seemed quite sure how the Egyptians used it. Some thought they made a sort of liquid, and soaked the bodies in a big vat for months. Others thought they used it dry, like talcum powder. Either way they left it for seventy days.

I used mine dry. For one thing, I didn't fancy leaving Jacqui soaking in the bath for more than two months. It's not that anyone would have found her. I could have used the top floor bathroom and locked the door. Besides, who was looking for her? Who cares about Jacqui except me? It's just that it seemed a grisly thing to do, having her lying in a bath, probably with a weight on her to keep her under.

I stuffed her full of natron. I dusted her all over, every niche and crevice of her. I filled up her insides, right up to her chest cavity where her lungs had been, right down to where I'd taken out her bladder and bowels. I packed all that solid.

I did the same with her head. I got pounds of it into her skull through her nose and filled up her eye sockets and mouth.

Her mouth was quite tricky. I had to get the natron right down her throat. That seemed a rotten thing to do.

Then I put two inches of natron in the box I'd made for her, put her in, filled it completely to the brim, and put the lid on.

I hoped that would be OK. I was really worried in case something went wrong and Jacqui started to rot.

I left her ten weeks like that, from February up to the beginning of spring.

I was glad the weather stayed cold all that time. Each time the sun came out, I'd start worrying. How the Egyptians managed in their heat I can't imagine. People must have dropped dead all the time on really scorching days in the desert, yet the embalmers there managed to preserve them successfully. I suppose I was lucky. I was only glad it was winter and the weather stayed cold and frosty right up to April.

I was careful not to wash her, that can stain the skin. They ruined the body of Saint Bernadette like that, by washing her. I learned that in a book I found on natural mummifications. Did you know people can turn into mummies spontaneously, without anyone preparing them or doing anything at all?

I saw one like that when I was in the British Museum. They call him "Ginger." He's a sand preservation. If you bury something in hot sand it doesn't rot, it just gets perfectly preserved. You can even do it with flowers. If you bury a rose in hot sand, it will stay perfectly preserved for years, just as fresh as when you picked it. Old Ginger's supposed to be thousands of years old, yet he's still got hair on his head. That's how he got his name, because his hair's red.

Another way you can get mummified naturally is by being left in a current of air. That sort of thing happens in the lofts of houses. You'd be amazed how many people have been found mummified in lofts. One time, someone found twelve babies like that. It seemed the woman of the house was an old maid, but she'd been having an affair with a married man and all the babies were born dead. She'd wrapped them in newspaper and put them in the loft, and they'd turned into little mummies.

Saint Bernadette was a natural mummification. She was buried in the ground in the regular way for years, yet when they dug her up they found she was absolutely perfect. Her skin was as soft and white as when she was alive. The book showed a photo, and she was really beautiful, with a lovely gentle face.

Then the nuns washed her, and the water made coffee-like stains on her skin. The nuns thought they were doing the right thing. They wanted to put her on show, in a big glass coffin on the altar of the church. (You can still see her, apparently, down in France somewhere. She's been dead well over a hundred years, but she looks as though she passed away yesterday, perfect except for the coffee stains on her.)

So I was careful not to wash Jacqui. I just dusted the natron off her skin with a new paintbrush.

I was cleaning up her hands when I found bits of skin under her nails. I realized right away that was bits of me, where she'd clawed me. I left them there. It gave me sort

258

of a nice feeling to think that a little bit of myself was being mummified along with her and the baby. It could be I'd be killed one day in the car, and Jacqui and little Eddie wouldn't be found for a hundred years. But no matter what happened to my body, there's still be a little bit of me with my family in the tomb.

I bought her another wedding ring, too, identical to the first one, and put it on her hand. It seemed the right thing to do, even though in the end it was all covered up by the bandages.

The last job was to pad her out, to fill up all the hollows I'd made in her body. The ancient Egyptians used resin and sand. I used foam chips like they put in cushions. I filled up her stomach with foam chips and got it all properly smooth and level.

And then I bandaged her all up.

That's harder than you'd think. You really need ten pairs of hands. You've got to pass the bandages under the body thousands of times as you go around and around the torso and legs. My first few layers weren't very tidy, but I got better, and my finishing turns would have got me a nursing degree.

The way I finally arranged it, I put Jacqui in her coffin on a couple of nice trestles I made, and put little Eddie in his bottle at her feet. On the glass, over Jacqui's face, I attached an enlargement of a photo, like a death mask. You could see the two of them through the glass top.

Whenever I went in, I'd switch the light on and have a look at them. It felt peaceful having them there, like going into a bedroom where someone you love, your mother, or your girlfriend, is asleep, and you tiptoe around and try not to wake them up. I kept hoping I'd be as well looked-after myself, when my own time came.

Of course, my job wasn't complete yet. The final thing to be done was to get her soul prayed for.

The Egyptians didn't make mummies out of people just for the fun of it. The idea was that you kept the body of the dead safe while you got prayers said for your loved one. That was the point of the whole ancient Egyptian religion. It was why they built the pyramids.

There's all kinds of silly explanations as to why they had the pyramids built. Some people think they were markers for redividing the land after the floods. Some think they were for watching the stars from, or built by spacemen.

Some even think they were for buying pharaohs in, which is about as daft an idea as you can get.

You take a people as brilliant as the ancient Egyptians, I mean really clever people who invent math, invent picture language, irrigation and all that, and then someone tries to tell you they were so thick as to spend fifty years and use millions of blocks of stone just to build a tomb for a dead king.

No, they built the pyramids to pray for their dead. That was their thing, what else would they have built them for? It's obvious enough when you look at them, at the way they were laid out.

There was the magic mountain in the middle. (All the ancient peoples thought the gods lived on magic mountains. Even the Christian God was always on the hilltops at the beginning, before Heaven was thought of.) Then there were the buildings with altars in them where the sacrifices were made and the prayers were said. Then the houses for the priests, and last of all, a big wall around everything, with a gate in it.

The way it worked was, you had to pay to be buried there, it was the customers' money kept the places going. The more money you had, the nearer to the middle was the grave plot you got.

Very poor people, who couldn't afford the fees to be buried inside, used to sneak up at night and bury their dead in the sand outside, just touching the wall. (Old Ginger was supposed to have been buried like that.)

When they dig around pyramids, you find all the big shots buried close to the base, princesses and prime ministers and people like that. Then further out, the more ordinary people like you and me.

That was how they got so big. There was a stupendous amount of money in them. Think, all the rich people of an empire were worried about their souls, and that went on for thousands of years!

You know how people never begrudge money to spend on themselves? They won't give then pence to a blind beggar, but they'll spend a fortune on health farms to get rid of their fat.

They've still got the same system going now. You take any cathedral close or even any country churchyard, and it's exactly the same model as the old pyramid complexes. There's the main building, with its magic mountain (only we call it a steeple), the altar to the gods, the priest and his offices. Then all around there's the dead people in the ground, trying to lie close to the magic mountain, where the power comes down from Heaven. The richest get the closest. You never saw a poor man's tomb, in one of the old churches, stuck right by the altar like the bigwigs, did you? The less cash you had in this world, the further away you were buried, until the really hard up, the paupers, were shoved right up against the churchyard wall.

No one is so poor these days that he's buried outside the wall, that's saved for suicides.

And dogs and cats. A lot of people still sneak up the churchyard at night and bury their pets touching the wall.

There was nothing mysterious about the pyramids. They were built for the same reason people built big cathedrals. Think of the trouble someone thousands of years from now will have understanding somewhere like Salisbury Cathedral. Why on earth should someone build a tower five hundred feet high on a church, when it's only for people six feet tall to go into?

Now that I had finished my work of art and love (which is how I came to think of it), I found myself enjoying getting back to my taxi work on a regular basis, picking up people in one place and dropping them in another, them saying "Thank-you" and me saying "Thank-you" for the tip. One day this leathery-faced, ancient-looking man with a bit of an accent gets into the cab, and I keep looking at him in the rearview mirror, and finally I say, "Excuse me, sir, but by any chance are you an Egyptian?"

Well, he roars at me, "None of your damn business!" as if I'd insulted him, when actually it was intended as a compliment. I told him to get out of my taxi, right there in the middle of nowhere. I didn't want any money from him, I just didn't want to accommodate him anymore.

When he saw the murder in my eye he got out all right, but he shook his fist after me, shouting "I'll report you!" and made like he was writing down my number.

Chapter

They were a brilliant people, the old Egyptians. Half the ideas people have these days about religion and stuff came from them. The idea of the soul, that came from them. Heaven and Hell, they invented those, too.

They invented the resurrection of the body as well, the idea that some day God would put life back into all the people who'd died. Most people think those things are Christian, that Jesus thought them out. But the ancient Egyptians invented them thousands of years before Jesus was even a twinkle in God the Father's eye.

But it's not easy to get someone's soul prayed for these days. Not once they're dead. Anyone will do it while you're alive, when you can look after yourself and don't need it.

They used to pray for the dead in the old monasteries in England, before the time of Henry the Eighth. But they've changed all the religions these days. It's all Yankee cults now. No wonder hardly anyone goes to church. Once upon a time, so many people went to church that they built huge cathedrals for them. Now you can fit the whole lot into a tin hut.

Once, I tried to sound out a guy in a church about it, but he thought I was mad.

Then, there was this old girl my firm drove to services every Sunday morning, and one day I got given the job. I had to take her to this little chapel with "Jesus Saves" stickers plastered all over the front, and after the minister had helped her out of the car and this other woman had taken her inside, I got nattering with him.

We were both keen to get to know each other. I wanted to find out about this praying-for-the-dead business, and he wanted to convert me so he could get more money on the collection plate.

I had to let him chatter on a bit first about why didn't I come inside and be saved, before I could get my question in. And when I did, it was just a waste of time. He was an idiot. He nearly hit the roof when I asked him about praying for dead people. (I didn't mention Jacqui, I just brought it up in a general way.)

"That's not Christian," he said, "that's just rank superstition."

What the hell did he think all his cymbal banging and

shouting "Hallulujahs" at the tin roof was, then? I suppose he thought that was rational twentieth-century behavior.

And then I saw this program on TV one night about this monastery in Egypt that had been there for thousands of years. It sort of went right back to the beginning of things, not like the religions we get in this country, which were only all invented the day before ycsterday.

I thought, "If anyone knows anything about real religion it's got to be these guys. They learned all the proper stuff, from when it all started. They didn't start making it all up at the time of Henry the Eighth."

I wrote off to this place and told them I wanted my wife prayed for, that I wanted them to pray her soul would be OK. I told them a little lie and said she was in the family vault. I wanted them to know her body was being looked after, that things were being done properly.

I was a bit worried because I sent it in English and I wondered if they could translate it. I put some money in it, too. I didn't know if they used money, but I got a special draft from the bank and made a donation, just like with the priests in the pyramid temples.

One evening I came in from work and there was this letter waiting for me, with interesting stamps on it. It was from the monastery. The abbot himself had written back to me, in English. It was a really beautiful letter. It said,

> Dear Sir,
>   The Brothers and Priests here will remember your dear wife and child in their prayers, that their souls may be

received into Paradise. Your generous donation is most gratefully accepted. We wish you every blessing of God.

It gave me a tremendous warm glow inside to think the abbot of this great big monastery would write me a personal letter and that all these monks, way out in the desert, would be praying for Jacqui. I felt like going back to that idiot in the tin hut and shoving the letter up his nose. What bloody frauds those guys are, setting up churches when they don't know a damn about religion!

But I didn't want to waste my beautiful letter on him. I put it in with Jacqui and the baby instead. I found a little jewel box in my mother's old room, and I put the letter in it and put the box at the end of Jacqui's coffin. That seemed the right thing to do with it, putting something from some really holy person in with her.

Her soul went all sort of peaceful and happy after that. I could feel it talking to me. Not in words, souls don't talk in words. But I could feel Jacqui thanking me for taking the trouble I had. She was thanking me for not just chucking her body away, for caring for and protecting herself and her little son. I closed the secret door on their room and the house felt quiet and peaceful, like an honest church.

But I still had one worry on my mind.

Chapter

What would happen to Jacqui and Eddie when I died? I suppose every bloke worries about his family like that. No man likes the thought that one day he'll be helpless to help his wife and children.

It can happen anytime. Death can come to a man any hour in his life, whether he's young or old. If you drive a thousand miles a week like I do, it could very easily come in the car. Not a week goes by without me seeing an accident on the road, though they say high-mileage drivers like cabbies hardly ever have accidents. It's the tear-asses and the guys who drink in the evenings who cause ninety percent of all the smashes. But there's still that other ten percent.

Or you could die of natural causes.

My mother died like that. It was just after I started work taxiing, and I came home one afternoon and found the police had left a note in the door asking me to go to the station, and when I got there they told me all about it. She was taken bad out shopping, and when the ambulance got her to the hospital she was already gone.

She'd had a stroke. She'd just thrown her hands up to her head and collapsed. It's the sort of thing can happen to anyone.

Who knows what's going on in his own body? Right this minute there might be a clot heading for your own brain, and you're just sixty seconds away from a stroke. Or your heart might just be saying to itself, "Right, that's enough pumping then, knock off now," and ten seconds later you're on the ground breathing your last.

I saw that happen while Jacqui was away in Wolverhampton. I was out on a job, doing a parcels run, and I'd just stopped to buy a couple of magazines when I saw a woman drop dead in the street right in front of me. She just keeled over. There wasn't a mark on her. She wasn't old or overweight or sick looking or anything, her time had come, her body had given out, the same way it will with all of us.

You don't get any warning. All the time I was trying to help this woman (all I could do really was put my magazines under her head to keep it off the pavement), her friend who was with her kept trying to pull her to her feet.

"Help me get her to her feet," she kept saying. "She'll be all right. She just slipped."

But she was dead all right. She had that terrific looseness about her, as though she'd been fileted and all her bones taken out. Even when the ambulance finally came, her friend didn't believe it. She was in tears. "She must be all right," she kept telling everyone. "We just had a cup of tea together."

You could see that. It was running out of her mouth every time her head rolled sideways. But she was still dead, the way we'll all be one day.

I stopped worrying about it. I stopped thinking about dying. There wasn't really anything I could do about it. If I died suddenly somewhere, all I could hope was that no one would start knocking the house about. Jacqui and my boy Eddie could be safe there for centuries, until the house was demolished or World War Three started and everyone got annihilated together.

I wondered what people would think, if they found the tomb a hundred years from now. Books would be written about it. They'd call them *The Case of the Mummified Mistress* or *The Woman in the Wall*. No one would know who Jacqui was. That made me angry. If the papers had paid more attention, I'd have clippings to leave with her for the people who'd need to know. I thought to put a letter in with her, explaining everything. But it would take a whole book to make it clear. A letter would just confuse things, it was better to let them find Jacqui. The Mystery Woman Who Was Loved.

My other worry was about the police. I hadn't heard from them for ages, but you could bet this business would still be in their files. Obviously, Jacqui hadn't been found, and they'd still be following up clues as to where she was. It might occur to them to come rummaging through the house again.

I didn't think for a minute they'd find Jacqui, her tomb was too well hidden. But I wasn't taking any chances. It made me sick to think of the sorts of things they'd do to her if they found her. They wouldn't leave her lying peacefully where she was. Not on your life! They'd take her out of her coffin in her own little room and have her lying naked on a dirty slab in some public mortuary. They'd hack all her bandages off her and start cutting her apart to satisfy their bloody morbid curiosity. When they'd finished, they'd probably use her as an exhibit in some medical school, put her in a glass case and have people poking at her for the next hundred years.

And as for little Eddie, Christ knows what they'd do to him. They'd probably just throw him in the incinerator or give him to the hospital cat. Doctors in hospitals murder thousands of helpless little babies like him every year when they do their abortions. They'd treat him like they would a pound of tripe. They'd think no more of throwing my little son in a furnace than they would of burning an empty candy wrapper.

I wasn't going to let them treat *my* family like that. The first thing I thought was I'd blow it all up. Like in the

276

pictures. They turn a switch and the whole thing goes "wham!" But I didn't know anything about explosives. And where would I get the dynamite for the charges? And what would it be like, living in a house that might go "bang!" any minute?

So what I did instead was leave a five-gallon drum of kerosene in the living room. I kept it full, and just sat a cup upside down over the neck. Then I put a little table over it with a long cloth hanging down so no one could see it under the table. And on the drum I put a box of matches, just ready. If the police came around and found anything. I could have the house like an inferno before they could move. I'd just pick up the matches, kick the tin over, and put a lighted match to the kerosene the second it hit the carpet. There's no way they could get the fire out till the place was in ashes.

I had this little deathbed scene in my mind. There's me, really old now, and I know I'm dying, so I want to protect my family, I don't want people banging around and finding my wife and child, so I crawl out of bed and set off my tin of kerosene. It must be rough, burning yourself alive, but I think I could do it for the sake of Jacqui and little Eddie. I wouldn't be happy dying and leaving them behind. I'd have the feeling I'd abandoned them, left them in danger. They'd be better off if I took them with me.

And that was it, really. When I had everything done, I settled down into my usual way of life.

When you do cabbing, you don't really need a social life anyway. You're just glad to be on your own and breathing clean air for a few hours. You often don't finish work till the early hours of the morning, and when you get back to the house it feels really wonderful. It's so quiet, and things stand still. And everything's so clean compared to cabbying, which is scruffy. Even if you clean your car up and put an air freshener in it, your next fare's a couple of smokers who stink it up again.

The office is always scruffy, too. Everyone chain-smokes, so there's always a stink in there. Even the telephone's sticky. No one ever cleans anything, so the whole place is covered with a layer of dirt.

You can see why getting back home's always a pleasure to me.

To tell the truth, with Jacqui and Eddie there, the house felt even more homey than before. It was like when my mother was alive. A house is always much better if there's someone you love in it.

I often went into their little room, just to dust around and look at them. I was careful never to leave tracks on the carpet or to spoil the fit of my secret door. I was careful, too, to lock all the doors and draw the curtains before going into my family's room. There was just a chance that someone might accidentally see me going in there and report it to the police. The silly bugger would probably think he was being public-spirited and decent, he wouldn't realize what a stupid, criminal thing he was doing.

Of course, I'd rather have them alive. But they weren't alive, so I had to count my blessings in other directions.

You get a lot of blokes, like I said, whose wives have

got pictures of film stars stuck up around the house, and they think more of the film star's picture than of the man they're married to. I was better off than the likes of them. My wife would never go off with another bloke, and my little boy would never leave me. You take the average married bloke, he lives in fear. He gets married and he slaves away for years building up a family, and all he sees at the end of it is himself living dead lonely, everyone gone away.

The kids will leave him as soon as they get big enough. He sees them shooting up every year, and before he knows it they're gone. He'll be lucky after that if he sees them once a year. And the wife gets bored and fed up with cooking and house cleaning, and as soon as the kids are off her hands she's having an affair with some guy.

I really felt happier the way I was. I know it sounds mad. I know if I was caught they'd try to take me away and lock me up in an asylum. But the thing was, I felt peaceful in myself, really relaxed and well. Every morning when I woke up I felt something like bliss. I'd see the sun coming in through the French windows and listen to the birds in the garden, and I don't think I've ever felt so good in my life before. All the little noises in the kitchen sounded like when you're on holiday and really enjoying yourself. Food tasted really delicious again. When I was out doing the garden, I'd stop and get a real buzz out of just watching a bee looking for whatever bees look for in the woodbine. Or I'd watch little drops of water shivering on the leaves, turning all sorts of colors in the sun.

When summer came, I put little Eddie's swimming

pool into commission. It was a very hot summer that year and I spent a lot of time splashing around in the pool. I got a really beautiful tan, and everyone started telling me how fit I looked.

One day, I was in the pool when the tecs showed up right beside it. I hadn't heard the bell, and they'd come around to the back on their own, looking to see if I was in the garden. I couldn't decide whether to talk to them from the water, or get out. Either way, I was at a disadvantage of sorts. I decided to get out and stand on their level, even though I don't look my absolute best in my bathing trunks. They asked me had I seen anyone suspicious around the neighborhood the past couple of days. It seemed there was a little girl down the road who'd been missing since before supper the day before. I told them I was sorry but I hadn't seen anyone, which was only the truth. And they could tell, of course, and they went their way, apologizing for interrupting my swim.

I found a new girl friend in July, too, or she found me, a girl called Tessa. She was a medical student. She was always reading medical books, and using me to practice on. Even when we were lying sunbathing by the pool she'd be feeling me to see how my muscles worked. I learned so much from her I could have been a doctor myself.

She was okay, Tessa. She wasn't perfect. Who is? But she did have really nice natural eyebrows, and she didn't have fancy nails. I often found myself thinking what a good mother she'd make if we had children together. I really fancied having children with her, it seemed a great idea.

I thought a dozen times of telling her about Jacqui and Eddie. Many an evening we'd be sitting together in the back sitting room with the French windows open on the garden and I'd imagine me saying, "Look, I've got something to show you." Then I'd go to my secret door in the paneling, open it up, and take her into the secret room to show her what was there. I thought, being a medical student, she would definitely be interested.

But I always changed my mind at the last minute. It wouldn't be fair on her. It's not the sort of thing you could expect a girl like Tessa to understand, even though she was smart and knew a lot about bodies. What did she know about souls?

I don't think it's the sort of thing *anyone* else would understand. Looking after your woman and kids is such a personal thing. It's everything to you, but it looks stupid to anyone else. You look at these families bringing up all kinds of kids gone wrong: mongoloids, cripples, really vicious delinquents, spastics, or just kids that are mean and stupid, and you ask yourself why they do it.

But they love them.

That's the way I felt about Jacqui and Eddie.

About the time I was embalming them, I happened to read an article in one of the women's magazines about Queen Victoria, our queen in the last century. She was married to this guy called Albert. She loved *him* so much that when he died she had the Albert Memorial built for him. That's that massive monument in front of the Albert Hall, with hundreds of statues all around it. If you built it today, it would cost you millions.

Victoria thought the world of Albert. After he died she never wore anything but black—for forty years—in mourning for him.

She absolutely adored *her* kids, too. She thought they had such beautiful little arms and legs that she had marble models made of them, and put in glass cases on show. Not models of the whole kids, just models of the arms and legs, as though they'd been cut off, all in glass cases, on velvet cushions. You can still see them in her old palace down on the Isle of Wight, just like they were over a hundred years ago.

Now, once upon a time I'd have thought the old lady was completely off her crust for carrying on like that. The magazine writer certainly did, she thought the old queen must have been barmy.

But I think I really understand Victoria. It strikes me that was a really nice, very loving sort of thing to do, by a very loving person. If you can't love your own family, then who *can* you love?

I thought when I read it, and I think now, we're two of a kind, really, me and Queen Victoria.

OTHER STEIN AND DAY BOOKS YOU'LL ENJOY:

			U.S.	Canada
	8064-1	**ASSASSINATION DAY** Kenneth Royce	3.95	NCR
	8042-0	**C.L.A.W.** Richard Graves	3.50	3.95
	8013-7	**DIRTY TRICKS** Chapman Pincher	3.50	NCR
	8019-6	**THE DUNKIRK DIRECTIVE** Donald Richmond	3.50	NE
	8084-6	**FALLS THE SHADOW** Emanuel Litvinoff	3.95	NCR
	8066-8	**THE GAZA INTERCEPT** E. Howard Hunt	3.50	3.50
	8032-3	**MAN ON A SHORT LEASH** Kenneth Royce	2.95	NCR
	8080-3	**THE RED DOVE** Derek Lambert	3.95	NCR
	8028-5	**THE RUN TO MORNING** Jack Higgins	3.50	3.50
	8052-8	**SIEGE** Edwin Corley	3.95	3.95

Buy them at your local bookstore or use this convenient coupon for ordering:

STEIN AND DAY/Publishers
Scarborough House, Briarcliff Manor, NY 10510
DEPT. SC

Please send me the books I have checked above. I am enclosing $ _____
(Please add .75 per book to cover postage and handling.) Send check or money order—*no* cash or C.O.D.s. Prices and numbers are subject to change without notice.

Name _____

Address _____

City _____ State _____ Zip _____

Allow 4-6 weeks for delivery.

STEIN AND DAY BOOKS

			U.S.	Canada
	8056-0	**THE BOOK OF GHOST STORIES** Peter Haining	3.95	NCR
	8012-9	**CASEBOOK OF A PSYCHIC DETECTIVE** Dixie Yeterian	2.95	2.95
	8044-7	**FIFTY TRUE MYSTERIES OF THE SEA** John Canning. ed.	3.95	NCR
	8094-3	**THE SIN EATER** Elizabeth Walter	2.95	NCR
	8047-1 (Occult)	**STAR SIGNS FOR LOVERS** Liz Greene	3.95	NCR
	8018-8	**THIS HOUSE IS HAUNTED** Guy Lyon Playfair	3.50	NCR
	8025-0	**YOUR PERSONALITY AND THE PLANETS** Michel Gauquelin	3.50	NE

MILITARY BOOKS FROM STEIN AND DAY

			U.S.	Canada
	8035-8	**ALL THE DROWNED SAILORS** Raymond B. Lech	3.95	4.50
	8015-3	**DEATH OF A DIVISION** Charles Whiting	2.95	2.95
	8109-9	**THE GLORY OF THE SOLOMONS** Edwin Hoyt	3.95	4.95
	8100-1	**A HISTORY OF BLITZKREIG** Bryan Perrett	3.95	NCR
	8039-0	**HOW WE LOST THE VIETNAM WAR** Nguyen Cao Ky	3.50	3.95
	8027-7	**MASSACRE AT MALMEDY** Charles Whiting	2.95	3.50
	8045-5	**ROMMEL'S DESERT WAR** Samuel W. Mitcham, Jr.	3.50	3.95
	8105-2	**SALERNO** Eric Morris	3.95	4.95
	8033-1	**SECRETS OF THE SS** Glenn B. Infield	3.50	3.95
	8093-5	**SUBMARINES AT WAR** Edwin P. Hoyt	3.95	4.95
	8037-4	**THE WEEK FRANCE FELL** Noel Barber	3.95	4.50
	8057-9	**THE WORLD AT WAR** Mark Arnold-Forster	3.95	NCR